The period of loan is normally three week

Edwardians at Play

SPORT 1890-1914

Edwardians at Play

SPORT 1890-1914

Brian Dobbs

PELHAM BOOKS

First published in Great Britain by PELHAM BOOKS LTD
52 Bedford Square, London WC1B 3EF
1973

© 1973 Brian Dobbs

ISBN 0 7207 0642 4

Set and printed in Great Britain by
Tonbridge Printers Ltd, Peach Hall Works, Tonbridge, Kent
in Garamond eleven on twelve point on paper supplied by
P. F. Bingham, Ltd, and bound by James Burn,
at Esher, Surrey

For my Father, an Edwardian and a sportsman

Contents

Illustrations

9

The Author and the Publisher wish to thank the following for permission to reproduce the pictures as indicated: *M.C.C. Collection* 4, 21, 23, 24, 27, 28, 29, 30, 31, 32, 33 *and* 34; *Mansell Collection* 1, 2, 6, 13, 22, 25, 36, 38, 39, 40, 41 *and* 50; *Press Association* 3, 10, 11, 19, 35, 43, 44 *and* 46; *Radio Times Hulton Picture Library* 5, 7, 8, 9, 12, 14, 15, 16, 17, 18, 20, 26, 37, 42, 45, 47, 48 *and* 49.

Acknowledgements

Research into sport of the Edwardian years would have been considerably more difficult without the massive contribution of the authors, statisticians and newspaper reporters writing during the period and since, and although it is impossible to make individual credits to all whose works and reports have been useful in some way or another in the compiling of this book, it is to the men who have had the urge to record their own and others' deeds on the field of play, that general gratitude should be expressed.

Thanks are also due to the staff of the British Museum Reading Room, to the staff of the Newspaper Library at Colindale, to the Borough Librarians and staffs of the Kensington, Camden and Westminster Public Libraries, and to the Editor and staff of *Sportsworld* magazine, all for help in tracing material mostly rare and out of print.

For particular permission to quote copyright material in the text, the author and the publishers would like to record their thanks to the following: to Brian Glanville and Eyre & Spottiswoode Ltd for the extract on p. 59 from *Soccer: A Panorama*; to the Rugby Football Union for the extract on p. 93 from *The Centenary History of the Rugby Football Union* by U. A. Titley and Ross McWhirter; to Major Rowland Bowen and Eyre & Spottiswoode Ltd for the extracts on p. 27 and p. 119 from *Cricket: a History*; to Sir Neville Cardus and Longman Ltd for the extract on p. 122 from *Cricket*; to Sir Neville Cardus and Cassell Ltd for the extract on p. 124 from *Full Score*; to C. L. R. James and Hutchinson Ltd for the extract on p. 124 from *Beyond a Boundary*; and to Leslie Duckworth and Hutchinson Ltd for the extract on p. 122 from *S. F. Barnes: Master Bowler*. If any other copyright has been infringed, the lapse has been wholly unintentional.

Acknowledgements

For assistance in obtaining photographs, the author and the publishers would also like to thank the *Radio Times* Hulton Picture Library, the Mansell Collection, the Marylebone Cricket Club (especially Stephen E. A. Green, Curator) and the Press Association (especially Mr Fred Adcock).

CHAPTER ONE

The Birth of Modern Sport

At 9 a.m. on Tuesday September 5, 1972, two thousand people cheered a volleyball match between West Germany and Japan. In horrifying contrast, four hundred yards away, eleven un-armed Israeli wrestlers, weightlifters and coaches entered on the last fifteen hours of their lives. By midnight they were dead, victims of Arab machine guns and hand grenades, victims of their own national identity, victims of savage barbarism spec-tacularly shocking even in a world where violent death has become commonplace, but most of all, victims because sport had become so commanding of universal attention that the assassins knew that their squalid and grotesque slayings were guaranteed maximum attention from the world's press and television media.

Not perhaps since the assassination of President Kennedy in Dallas in 1963, had there been an event to provoke so emotive a reaction in the heart of every civilised being in the world. September 5th 1972, the day of the Munich massacre, will re-main one of the blackest in history. Few would disagree with that, but I am convinced that the next day September 6th should also be remembered as the blackest day in the history of inter-national sport. On the morning of the aftermath, into the Olympic stadium filed 80,000 people to a hastily arranged memorial service. The Olympic flag and the flags of the 122 competing nations flew at half mast and the solemn strains of the funeral march from Beethoven's *Eroica* symphony echoed around the arena. In the half-religious, half-secular ceremony, Gustav Heinemann, the West German President spoke for many when he said 'We stand helpless before a truly despicable act'. Unfortunately, the International Olympic Committee and their retiring President Avery Brundage did not stand helpless for long. Before the day was over, and showing appalling insensi-

15

tivity to the feelings of the Israeli nation and the survivors of the Israeli team, Olympic competition was back in unseemly full swing. And before even the memorial service had been allowed to draw to a respectful close, Mr Brundage in his address had managed to equate the threatened boycott of the Games by the black African nations if Rhodesia was allowed to compete, with the bloody and terrible events at Furstenfeldbruck airport and the Olympic Village, as if they were of broadly the same character.

As a final unpleasant twist, this crass juxtaposition and his announcement that the Games would continue, were both greeted with prolonged applause by many of the mourners present. Meanwhile, unseen and unpublicised, some Norwegian and Dutch athletes packed their bags and departed, having lost all taste for sporting competition in the two days horror. They, one feels, were among the few present who had not forgotten that there were other things in life besides sport. Clearly there is much logic in the view that the Games had to go on lest Arab terrorism should have had the added satisfaction of ending them. That they should have gone on before the Israeli nation and world Jewry had had chance properly to mourn their dead was unforgivable.

Though this is the most spectacular example of sport taking precedence over all other considerations, it is by no means the first. Leaving aside the naïvety of those who believe that a rugby match or a cricket test with South Africa will in some mysterious unspecific way alleviate the evils of apartheid, there has been a school of thought that not only is sport not subject to the ethical considerations applying to any other human activity, but on occasion is even superior to life itself. As Thomas Hughes suggested in *Tom Brown's Schooldays,* to play rugby football was to enter a higher plane altogether, where 'one straining, struggling half-hour (was) *worth a year of common life'*. (My italics). The lingering power of such views can be amply demonstrated by the fact that to many athletes and sportswriters, the crimes at Munich were regrettable not for their offence against humanity, but because they interfered with the real business of the day – Olympic competition, training schedules, et al.

Some of those present, notably Neil Allen of *The Times,* Chris Brasher of *The Observer* and John Rodda of *The Guard-*

ian, spoke out courageously and gave great attention to the moral issues involved at Munich. To others, the meaningless cliché that politics should not be allowed to interfere with sport was yet again sufficient to cover the situation. I have said that Munich was by no means the first occasion when such naïvety has triumphed. In Melbourne in 1956, despite the ruthless quashing of the Hungarian uprising in Budapest, and the Suez debacle, the Games went on. In Mexico in 1968, some 200 demonstrators in the Place of the Three Cultures were mown down, but the Games went on. Perhaps the only confident prediction which one can make of the Olympics in Montreal in 1976, is that whatever extremists and lunatics do there in the magnetic spotlight of world-wide publicity, the Games will go on.

As Alex Natan once put it in a hard hitting essay on 'Sport and Politics', so many millions have been invested in the Games that cancellation would cost still more irreparable financial losses than were actually incurred in their continuance. He also said;

> It is significant that throughout the world the only people who deny the political nature of competitive sport are those whose livelihood depends on such lies, who are more interested in holding their positions in international sports organisations.

I wish this were true. If it were only those he mentions, perhaps the force of public opinion might force some radical changes. I suspect, on the contrary, that it is a view held by the majority of spectators at sporting events, and that straw polls taken in the restaurants, tea-rooms, and bars at Wembley, Wimbledon, Twickenham and White Hart Lane would produce ample evidence to support my view.

I believe, moreover, that in sport as in many other fields, the child is father of the man. There now seems a consensus of opinion that Munich 1972 embraced massacre, political demonstrations, doping illegalities, quarrels, violence, excessive patriotism, evasion of amateur rules, and protests by the score, because the £300 million pounds spent had created a Frankenstein's monster beyond the control of its masters. Many distinguished and intelligent men, David Hemery, Lord Killanin, the Duke of Edinburgh and Dr Roger Bannister among them, have endorsed this view. It is at least half true, but it conceals, in its

17

emphasis on the present, that Munich was the Olympic movement in the first stages of its senility, demonstrating with striking
and horrifying results, strains and stresses which had been present
from its birth in 1896.

The modern Olympics were born in the years between 1890
and 1914 which are examined in this book. During that twenty-
five years, sport moved into a new era. It exercised men's minds
and bodies to an unprecedented extent. It began, before the era
ended, to command the acres of newsprint it does today. It drew
participants and spectators as never before. It provoked argument, controversy and examination. Its followers clicked turnstiles, predicted and dissected results, bought sporting newspapers, magazines and books as they poured from the presses.
Sporting victories were looked on as confirmation that God was
an Englishman smiling benignly as the sun never set on the
vast territories where Pax Britannica held its sway; and sporting
defeats were gloomily held up as convincing proof that a tide of
national decadence and physical deterioration was in full spate.

Easy as it is now to smile at the Edwardian Jeremiahs who
saw physical and moral degeneracy in English failures to assert
traditional supremacy on fields of play, we cannot afford to be
too superior. When the England soccer team lost to West Germany at Wembley in 1972, there was sufficient concern to provoke
Parliamentary questions! This is a small example of the part
sport has come to play in our national life. It is just one of
many. We have all heard, to take another random example, of
factories where production has dropped dramatically after the
home team has been beaten in an important match.

From 1890 to 1914, sport grew to a peak of importance from
which there has been no retreat. On the contrary, it has, in one
sense at least, gone on from strength to strength. It is one of the
most powerful legacies left us by our Edwardian fathers and
grandfathers, yet conventionally how much attention does its
history get? The answer must be, precious little. It has suffered
on two counts.

Firstly, the sportswriter employed by a newspaper has to be
concerned with the transient and the fleeting. To a man feeding
the voracious appetite of the daily deadline, the Fleet Street
cliché – 'There is nothing so dead as yesterday's headline' – is
more than a cliché, it is a motto by which he has to earn his

bread and butter, or he will not earn his bread and butter for long. Secondly, the economic and social historian, far better placed to take a long term critical view, has tended to regard sport as a subject unworthy of academic attention. The standard social histories give sport, and that usually means only association football, a few sentences or ignore it altogether.*

The result is that most men's knowledge of the history of sport stems primarily from the days they watched or played themselves – conventionally in their childhood and youth – with their own fallible if colourful memories heightened by perhaps equally colourful and fallible memories passed on to them by their fathers and elders by word of mouth. Unblessed with the capacity for total accurate recall, most of us remember what we want to remember. As the years pass, the great goal, the thrillling try, the fast century, get ever greater, ever more thrilling and ever faster. The tedious midfield battle, the interminable infringements and the four hours of rain-interrupted play that preceded the goal, the try and the hundred have been forgotten because there was no reason to wish to remember them. Like any Romantic, when we recall the events of yesteryear, we like to put the heart before the coarse.

Most of the time, this essentially human reaction to the sport of the past is a harmless indulgence, a healthy desire to recapture and resavour pleasures gone by, but it can on occasion do more harm than good. It can do so in two ways.

If a contemporary sportsman is expected to conform to standards of excellence in conduct and performance that have never *actually* existed outside the fallible store of our memories, and the exaggerated glories of the past are used as a stick to chastise the failings of the present, this cannot be wise or fair. Secondly, and more seriously, if we totally neglect the past, and try to define and solve the many critical problems which sport now faces without reference to either how the problems started or to what solutions have been propounded in the past, our answers may be doomed to failure.

*There are, of course, some splendid histories of individual sports—H. S. Altham or Rowland Bowen on cricket, Dr Percy Young or Morris Marples on association football for example – but, with the exception of Peter McIntosh's pioneering *Sport in Society*, there is no overall view of trends in sport in a social and historical context.

To draw a not wholly irrelevant parallel, few would imagine that the strife and bloodshed of Northern Ireland will be halted without reference to the grievances buried in her constitutional, political and economic history; yet there are many who would seek to solve the problems facing the Olympic movement as if they began only at Munich.

Naturally, if history could always provide a satisfactory answer to a contemporary problem, there would be more historians and less politicians. Leaving aside the consideration that that might not be a bad thing anyway, there seem cogent reasons why it is time to take a closer look at the Edwardians than anyone has yet done.

In their determination to preserve the best of British sport, the Edwardians erected some elaborate administrative shelters to keep out the chill winds of social change and the driving rains of economic progress. That the winds could not ultimately be rebuffed, or the rain returned from whence it came, was not their fault. Their shelters were effective in their day. Since those times the shelters have become increasingly ineffective. We have replaced a brick here, repaired a slate there, but it becomes ever more apparent that the roof is leaking badly and the walls let in far too many uncomfortable draughts. And instead of recognising that the time has come for wholesale structural repairs at least, and more probably demolition and reconstruction, we have slapped on preservation orders and continued to shiver.

(And so, every four years, every Olympic competitor gives silent acquiescence to the Oath intoned on his or her behalf 'that sport to me is nothing more than a recreation without material gain of any kind direct or indirect . . .' Who then can say that hypocrisy died with the Victorians?)

It can be argued that 1890 to 1914 is too all-embracing a period to talk accurately of 'Edwardians', and admittedly Edward VII did not reach the throne until 1901 and was replaced by George V after his death in 1910. However, we are not examining politics and asking who opened the despatch boxes or gave the Royal Assent to Bills. So far as sportsmen looked for a lead in 1890, they looked to Edward, the Prince of Wales. By then, the Heir Apparent was Patron of the Rugby Football Union, Patron of the Surrey County Cricket Club, and Patron of the Football Association, and he became a leading racehorse owner throughout the Gay Nineties.

By 1890, sport was an almost obligatory interest of leaders of society. This was not always so. In a letter to his mother sent from Malta in 1830, Disraeli told her how he had once been in the gallery of a rackets court where he was struck by the ball which then lay at his feet. Elegantly dressed as ever, his response was to hand the ball to a rifleman standing nearby. 'I humbly requested him to forward its passage into the court, as I really had never thrown a ball in my life'. By 1890, no British Prime Minister, whatever his private feelings, would have made so damaging and 'un-English' an admission.

Edward may have been short, fat and balding, but he personified affability and jauntiness, with the confident and appealing air of a man attracted to the pleasures of the flesh and prepared to enjoy them. His geniality contrasted so strongly with the ageing widow Victoria in prolonged and solitary mourning since her bereavement, that inevitably sporting society looked not to Her Majesty but to Good Old Teddie. It was said in 1904, 'there is scarcely a game or diversion dear to Englishmen which the King has not himself either enjoyed or else found pleasure in watching. He is, of all Englishmen, the complete sportsman'. When newspapers or periodicals ran the latest of that ubiquitous series 'Great Sportsmen of Our Time', they generally started with the Prince of Wales.

In 1890, the Great Sportsman was not the man who played three or four team games and could beat 12 seconds for the hundred yards, it was the man who moved in the flourishing circles of country house society, who rode to hounds, fished private salmon and trout streams, shot pheasants and grouse by the hundred, then retired to the table to restore his lost calories at meals of innumerable courses and of a size that we would find gargantuan.

Significantly, the subject catalogues of reference libraries like the British Museum and the London Library for the 1890's which include the subject 'Sport' use it as a heading to cover huntin', shootin' and fishin'* and one has to look under 'Athletics and athletic sports' to find sport in its more modern sense. It is a measure of the changes of the years under dis-

---

*The English penchant for blood sports was nicely captured in a 1908 *Punch* Cartoon. A convalescent child says – 'I'm much better now, Nurse. Will you please put me at the window? I feel I could kill a fly'.

cussion that by 1914 it would have been C. B. Fry, cricketer, athlete, rugby and association footballer, who would be more likely to be afforded the title of a great sportsman.

In the same way that many of our present attitudes to sport and its conduct at all levels owe much to the rich legacy left us by the Edwardians, so they themselves owed much to what had gone before, and it is impossible to understand what they did and how they felt without reference to earlier times, and in particular to the massive contribution of the public schools.

I am indebted to T. C. Worsley's *Barbarians and Philistines,* an incisive examination made in the late 1930's, and to David Newsome's *Godliness and Good Learning,* for much that follows. The impact upon society of the public school and the widespread dissemination of the values imparted to its pupils, may not at first glance be wholly relevant to a study of sport but in fact, no proper assessment can be made without reference to this thorny subject.

If we follow the example of Mr Worsley and adopt Matthew Arnold's famous division of social classes into the Barbarian or aristocratic, the Philistine or middle class, and the Populace or working class, it will assist us to come to some sort of terms with this confused and confusing issue. Despite, or perhaps because of, its political overtones, it is essential to our understanding of Edwardian sport. (Like Mr Worsley, Peter McIntosh in his short but invaluable book *Sport in Society* – the first to draw meaningful parallels between events and opinions on and off the fields of play – also adopted Arnold's terms.)

In their original form, public schools were what their name implies – they were genuinely public in the sense that they supplied an education for 'poor scholars'. As soon as it became necessary to take in fee-payers to supplement their income, the rich pupil soon drove out the poor. Probably by the end of the eighteenth century, any remaining poor boys had been driven out or were loftily ignored or mistreated by the fee-payers. At most of the schools a kind of Barbarian anarchy reigned – conditions were atrocious and bullying at an unprecedented height. So low had the schools sunk that from 1770 to 1790, history records that Winchester had three rebellions, the most serious of which had necessitated the calling in of the military to restore order.

Reform was desperately needed but instead of borrowing some

of the liberal education ideas of the dissenting academies, the Barbarians who controlled public school affairs opted for a different solution.

As a necessary background, we must remember that the social history of the nineteenth century is largely composed of the increasing wealth of the middle class bourgeoisie and their resulting struggles against the landed gentry – the Philistines against the Barbarians. Because the Philistines predominated in numbers ultimately they won politically, but during that lengthy process stretching over the century and after, they were adopted, taken in and absorbed by the Barbarians largely through the medium of the public school.

Lytton Strachey in *Eminent Victorians* identifies the sort of attacks made on the public schools early in the nineteenth century:

> From two sides, this system of education was beginning to be assailed by the awakening public opinion of the upper middle classes. On the one hand, there was a desire for a more liberal curriculum; on the other, there was a demand for a higher moral tone ... growing respectability was shocked by such a spectacle of disorder and brutality as was afforded by (Eton) ... 'The public schools', said the Rev. Mr Bowdler, 'are the very seats and nurseries of vice'.

Reform of the educational system came all right. It came with the injection of that most bourgeois of all virtues, respectability. It came, moreover, mostly at the hands of one man, Dr Thomas Arnold of Rugby.

Arnold was appointed Head of Rugby School in 1828. Its numbers and its reputation stood at a very low ebb. Being the sort of man he was, it was the moral side of the task which appealed to him far more than the intellectual. He made so spectacular an assault upon vice and immorality that the other crying need, an educational curriculum which forsook the traditional dependence on Latin and Greek and became relevant to a rapidly changing world, was quietly forgotten. His attitude to science, for example, was quite clear:

> Rather than have physical science the principal thing in my son's mind, I would gladly have him think that the sun went round the earth, and that the stars were so many

23

spangles set in the bright blue firmament. Surely the one thing needful for a Christian and an Englishman to study is Christian and moral and political philosophy.

When addressing his pupils, he listed his priorities;

I repeat now: what we must look for here is, first religious and moral principle; secondly, gentlemanly conduct; thirdly, intellectual ability.

The trouble was, the intellectual ability soon proved a bad third. As a result, an all round education, which might have produced a new libertarian class who could have alleviated the worst follies of the industrial age, remained unobtainable. Arnold's spectacular successes in grafting Philistine respectability to Barbarian roots muted and finally killed off the other telling criticism made against public schools; that their narrow concept of education was not producing men capable of mastering problems in the outside world for which Latin and Greek declensions were ineffective tools. As a result, the inadequacies of the Army and the Civil Service (recruited exclusively from the public schools) ruthlessly exposed in the blunders of the Crimean War, repeated themselves again in the Boer War and to a large extent in the First World War.

This might seem to be straying a long way from sport, but it has a direct relevance because of what happened to Arnold's ideas in subsequent years. We have seen that his philosophy did include intellectual ability as a necessary part of his declared intention to turn boys into men, Christian gentlemen at that. Coleridge had once used the word 'manly' in the sense of maturity, but the concept of manliness in terms of piety and good learning, became, as the years passed, distorted by Arnold's disciples in the Muscular Christianity school. Arnold had defended flogging because a gentleman was still expected to display the Barbarian virtues of courage and the ability to bear or inflict pain without flinching. It was precisely those virtues that a public school boy was now expected to display on the field of play.

The Muscular Christians, like Charles Kingsley, Thomas Hughes (the author of that eulogy to Arnold, *Tom Brown's Schooldays*) and the Reverend Leslie Stephen (the Cambridge don and rowing coach), interpreted 'manliness' in terms of athleticism, spartan habits and patriotism. To be effeminate, intellectual or un-English was to be unmanly. And as they distorted Arnold's ideas, so their own became changed and distorted, until there was hardly a public school in England which did not consider compulsory sport as essential. As David Newsome has said, 'Between 1860 and 1880, games became compulsory, organised and eulogised at all the leading schools'.

In Arnold's time, school games were unorganised, occasional and for fun. Arnold himself was not responsible for the introduction of compulsory games, although he is sometimes given the credit for it, but after him, games began to take on an importance they had never had before. As the Royal Commission on Public Schools said as early as 1864;

> ... the cricket and football fields ... are not merely places
> of exercise and amusement; they help to form some of the
> most valuable social qualities and manly virtues ...

It was a view which the heads of public schools like Bradley (Marlborough 1858–70), Temple (Rugby 1857–69) and Thring (Uppingham 1853–87), Warre (Eton 1844–1905) and many others, would heartily have endorsed.

The fascinating thing is, as T. C. Worsley has pointed out, that this new view of sport grew in strength in parallel with Imperialism itself. The games and especially the moral virtues with which they were now surrounded corresponded roughly with what was required in the outside world. In wars against hostile tribes who lacked weapons and organisation; dash, daring, loyalty, courage and endurance, all of them fostered on the field of play, were at a premium. The high priest of this connection between battlefield and playing field was Sir Henry Newbolt. In one of his most famous poems, *Vitai Lampada*, the philosophy that sport and war are of a kind could hardly be more clearly expressed. That a modern reaction to the following two stanzas is likely to be laughter should not blind us to the fact that at the time and for a long time afterwards they were taken very seriously indeed.

> There's a breathless hush in the Close to-night—
> Ten to make and the match to win—
> A bumping pitch and a blinding light,
> An hour to play and the last man in.

And it's not for the sake of a ribboned coat,
Or the selfish hope of a seaon's fame,
But his Captain's hand on his shoulder smote—
'Play up! play up! and play the game!'

The sand of the desert is sodden red—
Red with the wreck of a square that broke—
The Gatling's jammed and the Colonel's dead,
And the regiment blind with dust and smoke.
And the river of death has brimmed his banks,
And England's far and Honour a name,
But the voice of a schoolboy rallies the ranks:
'Play up! play up! and play the game!'

It was a seductive philosophy. The straight bat denoted the officer and gentleman. The three-quarter dash could be a prelude to a bayonet charge, and the forward dribble an overture to a combined assault on an enemy position. Unfortunately this was a state of affairs which did not last long. After 1901 and the end of the Boer War, there was less and less connection (and it had always been as tenuous as in the examples I have outlined) between the greatness of England and success at sport. However, despite this fact, unpalatable to many, more and more stress was placed on the crucial importance of sport, sporting success, and sporting conduct.

The tragedy was that as the first 14 years of the twentieth century brought ever increasing domestic and international problems, social, economic and political, the values imparted on the field of play did less and less to enable Edwardian Barbarians and Philistines to even recognise the nature of the problems, much less solve them.

As David Newsome has pointed out, the compulsory playing of team games and the fostering of loyalty and pride took on an increasingly strident note – 'this development reflected the opinion of the upper-middle classes who were saturated with imperialistic notions and who welcomed the spirit of aggresive patriotism which helped to allay their fears of German militarism and foreign commercial and industrial rivalry'.

His views are echoed by Major Rowland Bowen in his monumental *Cricket: a history*. To this segment of Edwardian society, cricket '. . . was "their" game, which enshrined the Arnoldian and bourgeois virtues of Victorian England', and their attitude to the game was 'all part of the business of preparing the young men of England for the "great game" . . . to come'. Rightly, he draws attention to the virulence of the anti-Germanism of cricketer Archie Maclaren expressed in an August 1914 issue of *The World of Cricket,* as symptomatic of the attitudes of these men.

Undoubtedly, football, cricket and so on can be and were used to foster loyalty, courage and discipline, but these are ambiguous qualities. What virtue is there in loyalty to false ideals, or courage and discipline shown in a bad cause? One has only to think of the courage, loyalty and discipline shown by the followers of Adolf Hitler, to realise the ease with which these qualities can be turned to perverse and unworthy ends.

I do not wish to equate Edwardian England with Nazi Germany. That would be absurd. I am merely trying to emphasise the dangers of a set of values that is too narrow to encompass wider issues, and suggesting, with Mr Newsome, that the Edwardian public school 'in its efforts to achieve manliness by stressing the cardinal importance of playing games . . . fell into the opposite error of failing to make boys into men at all'.

That there were excesses is certain. One has only to read Alec Waugh's novel *The Loom of Youth* published in 1917, to see a graphic account of the fundamental importance given to games at the average Edwardian minor public school. His hero Gordon was

> at once brought face to face with the fact that success lay in a blind worship at the shrine of the god of Athleticism . . .
> He who wishes to get to the front has to strive after success on the field, and success on the field alone. This is the way that the future leaders of England are being trained to take their proper place in the national struggle for a right and far-sighted civilisation.

Incidentally, the master Bull, graphically depicted in Waugh's novel, is generally believed to have been modelled on the England rugby player G. M. Carey, a master at Sherborne for thirty years. Another England rugby international, E. R. Mobbs died in the War when he led his men in a charge at the German lines by kicking a rugby ball into the air and rushing forward as if tacklers not machine guns faced him – a graphic example of a tragic attempt to equate sport with war.

As early as the 1860s, the moral values that could be inculcated by organised sport, having been thought the correct formula for the education of the sons of gentlemen, began to be applied to solving the problems of the working classes. Left alone, they might fall into the twin pitfalls of vice and idleness. Therefore, if only they could be encouraged to play games . . . So, what was thought suitable for his master was also thought suitable for Jack.

That so many of our Football League clubs owe their origins to nonconformist ministers and social workers who formed boys' clubs and groups to play football bears eloquent testimony the proselytising that went on. Originally these groups, in the words of Charles Booth in *Life and Labour in London,* meant '. . . obligatory attendance at a Bible-class being administered medicinally with cricket and football to take the taste away.' The Biblical studies soon died out, but the cricket and especially football, spread like wildfire and their implied moral justification with them.

Sport became a panacea for all ills, physical and moral. Mr Eustace Miles, following the success of his pamphlet *A Boy's Control and Self Expression* which he assured parents was 'Free from Unpleasant and Unnecessary Detail', published a new work, *Let's Play the Game* or *The Anglo-Saxon Sporting Spirit* in 1904.

According to Mr Miles, to carry on with a friend's wife was 'unsportsmanlike' and we could gain from games

> . . . a precious elixir of life, almost of perpetual youth . . .

Cricket for example, illustrated

> . . . such invaluable ideas as co-operation, division of labour, specialisation, obedience to a single organiser (perhaps with a council to advise him), national character, geography and its influences, arts and artistic anatomy, physiology and hygiene, ethics, and even – if the play can be learnt rightly – general educational methods.

Sport could even deal with some of the more offensive aspects of the urban slums. At Bermondsey, where the children had been 'rude, violent, dishonest, and singing undesirable songs shamelessly, or else indulging in some degrading habit or other',

28

a short period of organised games at the University Settlement had worked miracles and

> ... you will find that they have learnt courtesy and control on the one hand, self-expression and enjoyment on the other; and their simple and fair and graceful games, and their simple and ennobling and pretty songs have extended not only to other children in the neighbourhood, but also to the parents. Different songs are now sung even in some public houses of that part.

Sport then, in some magical way, was going to solve the growing problems of a society where the rich were getting richer and the poor were getting poorer. Slum housing, urban poverty, unemployment, nutritional inadequacies and their results could be obliterated if only the working classes, like the upper and middle, could be taught to 'play the game'.

It has been argued with a great deal of truth, that the public schools were the medium whereby the Barbarians had absorbed the Philistines into their own ranks throughout the nineteenth century, and certainly the success of the public schools in making young Tory gentlemen of Liberal fathers' sons was considerable. (Gladstone, that model of high Liberal rectitude, was considered sufficiently an arch fiend as to be once stoned by Eton boys). This fact goes a long way to explain what happened in society generally in the 1880s.

During that decade there were more and more disputes in industry, a growing number of strikes (in 1888 alone there were 509) a general marshalling of the disparate forces of labour, and riots and protest meetings by the score. 1886 saw the windows of London clubs smashed after a meeting at Trafalgar Square, 1887 was the year of Bloody Sunday, and 1889 the year of the great strike for the Dockers' Tanner. Against this increasing threat to the status quo of the 'haves' from the numerically superior 'have-nots', the Barbarians and the Philistines stood firm and united in a closing of the ranks.

These trends in the social history of the times leading up to the Edwardian period are germane to our understanding of Edwardian sport, for a very remarkable thing happened. Out of the humble acorns planted by those pioneers who had taken sport, particularly football, to the masses for their own moral reasons and for the masses' social benefit, grew a mighty oak whose rapid growth and formidable strength took its planters by surprise. Not only did the masses (Matthew Arnold's Populace) take to the game, they made it very much their own, or more accurately, they reclaimed it as their own. The cycle had turned full circle.

The eighteenth century and earlier game of the masses – an unruly and violent struggle between disparate armies with a ball between them (a kind of unholy amalgam between rudimentary rugby and association football) played in the streets and the fields in a wholly random fashion, had been taken up by the public schools and, in the urge for order and codification characteristic of the Victorians, given rules, laws, and a new coherence. In its new and improved form, the masses readopted it.

With the advantage of hindsight, it is easy to see why this happened. The process of the industrialisation of Britain and her transformation into the workshop of the world had had two major results. Work or the prospect of work had brought employees into large urban environments. Where once the majority of the population had worked and lived in the country, the balance had shifted spectacularly to the town. Also, alongside this development, with its tendency to sap an individual's sense of belonging to any community larger than the family, more efficient industrial processes in the factories tended to deprive the worker of opportunities to use skill and judgement in earning his daily bread. When successive legislation in the form of Factory Acts allowed for some leisure time away from the machine and the bench, there was a great demand, none the less real for being unformulated by those who felt it, for something to bring to a Saturday afternoon a richness to alleviate the stifling drudgery of the rest of the week. Football, for players, and even more for spectators, came to fill this yawning gap as perfectly as if it had been specially invented for the purpose.

It had everything. It was the cheapest entertainment around, it was full of skills from which the veriest simpleton could gain vicarious pleasure, and it created, in eleven readily identifiable coloured shirts, a team of heroes who with their feet and their heads, could articulate something of the unspoken feelings of thousands.

Some saw this phenomenon for what it was. F. E. Smith the

barrister and Conservative M.P., never notable for particularly progressive views, was nevertheless among them. In an article he wrote in 1911, he said this:

The poorer classes in this country have not got the tastes which superior people or a Royal Commission would choose for them; they have tastes for exciting amusements to divert and exalt their spirits after a hard week's work; they gratify such tastes healthily, cheaply, conveniently, and harmlessly on countless cricket and football grounds all over England.

Others were horrified at the latest manifestation of working class idleness. In *Scouting for Boys*, first published in weekly parts in 1908, Lord Baden-Powell lent his support. He drew upon the awful precedent of the Roman Empire which, according to him at least, had fallen because its people had been fed by the state to become unemployed wasters who 'frequented the circuses, where paid performers appeared before them in the arena, much as we see the crowds now flocking to look on at paid players playing football'. He went on:

Football in itself is a grand game for developing a lad physically and also morally, for he learns to play with good temper and unselfishness, to play in his place and "play the game", and these are the best of training for any game of life. But it is a vicious game when it draws crowds of lads away from playing the game themselves to be merely on-lookers at a few paid performers . . . thousands of boys and young men, pale, narrow-chested, hunched-up, miserable specimens, smoking endless cigarettes, numbers of them bet-ting, all of them learning to be hysterical as they groan or cheer in panic unison with their neighbours . . .

It should now be possible to see two major attitudes to the development of sport. Both were so powerful that not only did they make a powerful impact on the Edwardian era, but they have been so persistent as to survive the turmoils of two world wars and to continue right up to today. On the one hand, there was the view fostered by the public schools and disseminated by many a grammar and secondary school who mimicked them, that sport played for its own sake could impart a whole code of moral ethics, and make its exponents better people. On the other hand, there was the attitude, not often articulated but none the less powerful for that, that sport, for player and especially for spectator, filled a basic need in the lives of many in a particularly exciting and colourful way.

In one sense at least, the second attitude *was* articulated. Every penny and sixpenny piece that was paid out over the turnstiles was a vote, a vote for an organised professional entertainment, and a vote, moreover, as effectively and emphatically cast, as one placed in a ballot box in a referendum. And with the casting of these countless thousands of penny votes went some subsidiary but powerful demands. For the majority of spectators, the price of admission bought the privilege of standing on the terrace to watch their newly created heroes perform. It also, for ninety fleeting minutes elevated them from the role of wage-slave, to the novel and heady heights of employer. And like most poachers turned gamekeepers, they could be mightily demanding in the new role. They were prepared to laud their paid heroes to the skies, but if the heroes trembled or fell momentarily from the pedestal on which they had been placed, the condemnation was swift, loud and pitiless.

To men like the now ageing Thomas Hughes, this new form of professional sport was alarming. He called it 'the child of the railways, free Saturday afternoons and the popular press'. He was right about its parentage, but what disturbed him particularly was that this new child showed every sign of disregarding its elders' advice as to its present and future conduct. Instead of playing England's traditional games for their capacity to impart all the manly Christian virtues, here was a new, and hitherto disregarded, breed of men playing it seemed only for that most sordid of all reasons, money.

Is it not an odd phenomenon in our society that it is almost invariably true that the men who have quite sufficient money of their own to live comfortably, are also the ones to find activities carried out for fees or wages, sordid? There is nothing so effective as a private income in enabling one to take a moral stance. And moral stances taken against the new phenomenon of professional sport were legion throughout the late Victorian and Edwardian eras.

These moral stances, sometimes but not always hypocritical, were one thing. There were also the stances, usually dressed in a moral guise which provided a defensive covering for naked self-interest. This latter stance was taken by those for whom every-thing in the sporting garden was lovely. They played football, cricket, etc in the way they had been taught in school, because they loved the games and because they were imbued with the doctrine that this was a worthy and morality-inducing thing to do. They were also, and this is crucial, a privileged minority who could *afford* to play sports. And to keep sport 'pure', modelled as it was in their image, they erected a vast superstructure of laws and qualifications to keep the masses out of *their* garden.

Against the forces of economic progress and the advances of democracy, their leaders in the sports administrations have gone on ever since, making a useless piecemeal concession here, fight-ing a doomed rearguard action there, and wherever possible, burying their heads in the legislative sands in the vain and useless hope that unwelcome facts, if disregarded, will go away of their own volition. And so, the crucial question of amateurism and professionalism, which caused some spectacular upheavals in the Edwardian years, continues to plague us right up to today.

I have dwelt at length on the moral attitudes of a minority of sporting amateurs, and on the unspoken demands of the many, because the two factors, acting together, go a long way to explaining why sport, of all the leisure time activities, has had so many heart-searching dilemmas to face. Because it has meant so much to so many for so many different reasons, its pattern of growth has been artificially stifled. Consequently it has failed to reflect developments in society as a whole, par-ticularly on the amateur/professional question.

If we look at three other fields of leisure – music, theatre, and writing for example – we see a broadly similar pattern. 95% of exponents are spare-time dabblers, the other 5% are sufficiently talented (or at least sufficiently lucky!) to get enough attention from the general public to make them full-time professionals. They supply goods for which there is a clear demand and they reap the rewards. No one expects these professionals to forego their earnings, and equally, no one expects an amateur who is fortunate enough to have his novel accepted or his painting exhibited, to turn down the money to preserve his amateur status. And if he is good enough to progress all the way to a full-time professional, our blessings go with him.

The fact is that there are barely 5% of practising sportsmen who *could* either draw crowds or earn fees for their talents, but because they are the ones who receive 95% of the publicity, and because it is their doings which capture the public imagination, their every failing is put under a merciless microscope, and thereafter held up as convincing proof that excesses follow inevitably upon professionalism. That the conduct of professional sport in this country is overwhelmingly honest and examples of corruption notable for their scarcity, is less often stated. Lingering suspicions of professional sport are yet another facet of our legacy from Edwardian England.

Sport has grown throughout the world to a size and importance which an Edwardian would find baffling and alarming, but it is only the continuance of a trend which was strongly underway in his own times. The relevance of the years 1890–1914 to today is that it is possible to see in them the major trends in our sport in their early development. Sport, as we know it, was born in that quarter of a century. As our brief dip into Victorian education and social history has already shown, it did not spring up fully armed in 1890, but from then until the well nigh total suspension of sporting activities during the First World War, the major patterns of modern sport were set.

One of the surest indications of the growth in importance of sport during those years is its coverage in the newspapers. And, sure enough, sport's ever increasing attraction to players and spectators is duly paralleled in the columns. On January 5th 1891, *The Times* gave about a third of a column to a report of the Wales v England rugby international at Newport. The relative importance of the event can best be gauged by the fact that that day's issue of *The Times* also gave 1¾ columns to the weather, and not a few column inches to the Chancellor of the Exchequer's receipt of a 11s 4d postal order from an anonymous donor of 'conscience money'. By 1914, a rugby international was getting the sort of coverage we would expect today, and the sports sections of the dailies, even the august *Times* could be measured in pages rather than columns.

The Education Act of 1870 and its implementation of primary education in the three 'R's, had brought in its wake a new reading public. And as sport ranked as one of their major interests, it was eminently profitable to supply them with sporting news and views. Alongside the newspapers, there were hosts of new books –

textbooks, histories, annuals, ghosted autobiographies *et al* – and a truly phenomenal number of sporting magazines, many short-lived, but in retrospect, providing perhaps a more varied coverage of specialist interest then we can boast today. (Unlike the French, we cannot supply sufficient of a readership to support a daily all-sports paper like *L'Equipe*.)

One scholar, C. M. Van Stockum, in 1914, made an attempt at providing a bibliography of sporting books and magazines. His book, neither comprehensive nor accurate, failed miserably to encompass the field and he had to content himself with the vague statement that there were probably *at least nineteen thousand* items, and he had only covered the years from 1890 to 1912.

It has been estimated* that in 1896 there were 4,450,000 books in stock and by 1911 10,874,066, and that in 1901, there were 2,510 newspapers (516 in London) and by 1910 2,985 (734 in London). This latter figure does not include magazines of which there were between 1,000 and 2,000 titles in every year of Edward's reign.** These figures are for newspapers and magazines of all kinds, but they show dramatically that events in the world of sport were known more widely than ever before, and that sporting heroes had an unprecedently large following. They were the real-life equivalent of the glamorous white-limbed youths of the current sixpenny novels, with the same capacity to excite the imagination.

The sportsmen were also playing games we would readily recognise today. Despite the many advances in speed, fitness, tactics, and equipment over the last sixty years, which it would be idle to ignore, the games were in essence played much as they are today. In his examination of the unique series of soccer matches in *England v Scotland*, Brian James said

> The nineties make their impression not for their curiosity but rather for their familiarity; the most persistent attitude for the researcher into the period is delight at recognition.

His well chosen words could serve equally for the other sports too.

The quainter customs of Victorian sport – twenty a side rugby, hacking in soccer, round arm and under-arm bowling in cricket, and hour glass tennis courts, for example – had already died out.

*ed. Simon Nowell Smith, *Edwardian England*, p. 309.
**Ibid*, p. 320.

The difference between Edwardian and modern sport is one of degree rather than kind, and we should give them credit for being what they are, the fathers of modern sport.

It would be impossible for one man to read, let alone evaluate, all the source material available on the whole spectrum of Edwardian sport, and it would be equally impossible in this present work to treat every sport with the detailed attention which it deserves. In what follows, I have therefore concentrated mostly on four major topics, association football, rugby, the Olympic Games and cricket. This is because these four show in their development common trends, and trends which have their parallel to greater or lesser extents in the other sports. It is also, broadly speaking, giving these four the priority which the Edwardians themselves would have given them.

If this survey can either enable us to see current problems in the light of history and therefore better able to tackle those problems, or provide a starting point for others to examine more closely facets of the past which have been unjustly neglected, then it will have been worthwhile. It is a partial view, but, I hope, not one without a basis of truth.

So much of previous writing on the Edwardian sporting scene has been in the nature of a nostalgic look back to a vanished Golden Age, that to mention problems at all is to cut across a powerful trend of opinion. Bringing many of the forgotten conflicts temporarily back into the light, does not stem from any desire to denigrate the Edwardians. That the age had more fun than conflict, more grace than ugliness, and more emphasis on winning well than on the contemporary philosophy of first ensuring that one does not lose, is undoubtedly true. What I am concerned with, in re-telling some of the great deeds of the past, is that we do not forget to take an all-round view.

Sir Neville Cardus once wrote of '. . . hot days in an England of forgotten peace and plenty', and those words might serve as an example of the way the era has frequently been treated. What, if we are to be honest, we must not forget, is that although the sun shone, it also went behind the clouds as often and as maddeningly as today, that the 'peace' was tempered by an aggressive and restless desire for war among a vocal and significant minority, and that the 'plenty' was not shared out among the many, but jealously guarded by the few.

CHAPTER TWO

Football's Trials and Tribulations

A foreign visitor to London on a Saturday morning in April 1890 would have been baffled, as have many since, by strange accents emanating from Yorkshiremen and Lancastrians who wore scarves, favours and white and red roses, as they wended their way south of the river. If the visitor had bothered to consult his *Baedeker Guide to London,* an explanation would have been at hand, for amidst the references to London's many chess and billiard rooms, he might have spotted the invaluable information that 'Kennington Oval is the scene of the best matches under Football Association rules.'

It was F.A. Cup Final day and from the ranks of 132 clubs who had entered with hopes months before, three eliminating rounds and two semi-finals had left only two clubs optimistic of finishing the day in possession of the gleaming silver trophy. To give the annual battle an added piquancy, for the first time the match was a miniature Battle of the Roses, and, as twenty thousand people crossed one or other of London's bridges, eleven men representing Blackburn Rovers and eleven men of Sheffield Wednesday sat in their respective dressing rooms and prepared themselves for battle.

At the Oval, the gates were opened at 1.00 pm, although the kick-off was not to be until 3.30. In the Rover's camp, the team whistled and sang, cheerful in the knowledge that in their ranks were three survivors from the Blackburn teams whose Cup victories in 1884, 1885 and 1886 had wrested the balance of football power away from the Old Boy amateurs, and nine full internationals. That they were mostly recruited by some adroit scouting over the border in Scotland did not concern them any more than it concerned the thousands who had journeyed down from Lancashire to see 'their' team win.

For Sheffield, the Yorkshiremen present proudly pointed out that ten of their team were local Tykes. By 5 pm however, the gloom later reported in the Wednesday dressing room had spread to every Yorkshireman present. They went home cup-less after a moderate match at best and after a 6–1 thrashing. Blackburn's Townley scored a hat-trick from outside-left, one without bothering to cut inside before he shot, and veteran Lofthouse added the final goal from a corner to be enveloped by an over-enthusiastic section of supporters who invaded the pitch to celebrate. They were only removed after five minutes solid endeavour by the police and the military.

Wednesday's cup of woe was not, however, quite complete. Despite their appearance in the Final, they were still refused admittance to the Football League formed only two years earlier, a body which rubbed salt in the wound by black-listing them with Stockton and Ardwick (later Manchester City) in January 1891 for daring to try to seduce League players to their club (probably an inevitable result of the mauling they had received in 1890 by relying on their own resources). They were not to know then that the next decade would bring them a welcome to the Football League itself which they headed as Champions in successive seasons in 1903 and 1904. Dame Football, a jealous goddess, has been ever thus in her alternating frowns and smiles on her worshippers.

The League had been in existence but two years, and we shall have to examine its formation and growth more closely in a moment, but the 1890 Cup Final was the nineteenth of the series. It had come a long way since its inception in 1872, its first eleven years of existence being a Southern amateurs' monopoly broken by Blackburn Olympic in 1883. After that significant shift to the industrial North, the Cup was not to come south of Birmingham until the twentieth century, and even then only twice in twenty-odd years.

By 1890, the Cup was flourishing. To many, it *was* football, and although it had already solved many teething troubles, there were still lingering anomalies which demonstrated that its growth to its modern form was not yet complete. In 1890, Sheffield Wednesday in the Third Round had played Notts County three times, and not because they failed to achieve a result. They won the first game 5–0 but a Notts protest on some obscure point or other rendered the match void. They lost the second 3–2 but by protesting in their turn got that result cancelled. Whether either side protested after the third match, won 2–1 by Wednesday, is not known, but if so they must have been over-ruled for the result stood and Sheffield went on to beat Bolton Wanderers in the semi-final 2–1*. By then, the arbitrators must have been heartily sick of contests won and lost on the field merely to continue in the committee room. (In 1890, administrators had their other problems too – including a ticklish decision whether or not football on skates was legal! Unlikely as it may seem, they decided it was.)

Probably the most significant thing about the 1890 Final is the fact that it was played by two professional teams and that they were from two industrial strongholds. Football's phenomenal growth in previous decades was bearing fruit. We have already seen in the last chapter some of the reasons why this happened, so it is no surprise to see that professional clubs grew first in the most fertile soil of all – that of the large Northern and Black Country industrial complexes – Yorkshire, Lancashire, the Midlands, and the North East – where all the economic and social factors were going for it.

Although the 1880s are, strictly speaking, outside the period covered in this book, we must examine them briefly, for the growth of football, which inevitably brought professionalism in its wake, was a development which was to come to other sports, and it was to football that other sports administrators looked when they came, in their turn, to grasp the thistle of the amateur/professional question. For every one who praised the Football Association for their pioneer efforts, there were ten who condemned them as an awful example of the corruption which would inevitably follow if money were allowed to intrude into sport. The most common tendency was not to look to the F.A. and learn to correct what errors they did make, but rather to condemn them out of hand. It is only today that one can look back and say that considering that the football administrators of the 1880s

---

*Even that is not as simple as it sounds, for in a second half played in driving rain, all three goals were scored and vigorously disputed, and Bolton 'scored' a disputed equaliser which looked to many present much fairer than the three allowed to stand. Who can say that arguing with referees is exclusively modern phenomenon?

were trying to find solutions for unprecedented problems, tardy as they were to face the facts, they sometimes did rather better than they could reasonably have been expected to do.

Even before 1880, many of the Northern clubs were making compensatory payments to their players for out-of-pocket expenses on match and training days, and where a player was losing part of his week's wages to fulfil the needs of the club, solace in the form of hard cash found its way into his pocket. As crowds grew and the takings at the gate increased, this seemed to many to be equitable and fair, and it took a very slight adjustment to form the further opinion that the gate money would be larger yet and the team even more an attraction, if better players could be obtained. And what better inducement to the recruitment of these better players than the payment of cash?

At this time, the average English player was a dribbler, an individualist whose basic idea of the game was to put his head down and head for the opposing goal. If he was tackled, he and the attack were stopped, and that was that. It seems never to have occurred to him that the team-mates running alongside him might be better placed to continue if only he passed the ball to them when he was faced with a tackler. That was just not done.

In fact it was done, but only across the border in Scotland. There a close-passing game had been developed on the eminently sensible philosophy that there was no point in being upended by a hefty defender if the ball could be given to a companion a few yards away before that unwelcome event took place. Some put the prevailing English philosophy down to pure selfishness, others have since suggested that self-reliance was more what was intended. Either way, it could be called the Stupid Method and the Scots at international level offered conclusive proof that their's was the more constructive of the two battle-plans. The results of the England v Scotland matches from 1876–1884 (the series started in 1873) were, England's scores first, 0–3, 1–3, 2–7, 5–4, 4–5, 1–6, 1–5, 2–3, 0–1 respectively.

The clubs of the North looked, marvelled and did something about the trend – they began to recruit Scotsmen. Between 1879 and 1882, led by Blackburn Rovers and Darwen and soon followed by Preston North End and Bolton Wanderers, the English clubs, proffering the twin baits of a place in their team and a

well-paid job in their area, lured the most skilful Scottish players
to their ranks.

The infiltration did not go un-noticed but for the moment
officialdom was reluctant to give any indication that they had
noticed what was going on. C. W. Alcock, the Honorary Secretary of the Football Association and practically the inventor of
the F.A. Cup competition, referred uneasily to the developments
in the North in his *Football Annual* of 1881, but nothing further
was done.

Then, in 1882, the F.A. Committee passed a new rule that:

Any member of a club receiving remuneration or consideration of any sort above his actual expenses and any wages
actually lost by any such player taking part in any match,
shall be debarred from taking part in either cup, inter-
Association, or International contests, and any club employ-
ing such a player shall be excluded from this Association.*

In the light of what *was* happening in some clubs, even King
Canute could not have passed a more ineffective resolution. As
the recreation of the few had become the mass entertainment of
the thousands, the tide was not to be stemmed by such feeble
piety.

By October of the same year, a Special Committee had met
and appointed a seven-man commission to inquire into the
'rumoured importation and payment' of players. The commission
met, 'investigated', and at a time when some Lancashire clubs
saw as many haggises as footballs, reported in February 1883
that there was not sufficient evidence available to reach firm
conclusions. Poor Accrington Stanley were expelled from the
Football Association in November 1883 for paying one of their
players, but with that single scapegoat the Association contented
themselves, and Accrington went temporarily into the wilder-
ness for doing retail what others were doing wholesale.

There, one supposes, is where matters would have rested but
for a January 1884 Fourth Round cup-tie between Preston North
End and Upton Park. Unhappy at a draw against a side which
could reasonably have turned out in kilts, Upton Park protested

*Quoted in Geoffrey Green's *The Official History of the Football Association*,
p. 97. The relevant details of minutes of other F.A. meetings quoted in this
chapter can also be found in this essential history.

the result on the grounds of Preston North End's 'professionalism'. The following week, an Upton Park official and Major Sudell of Preston attended a Committee hearing at the Oval.

Sudell's bluff honesty soon dispelled any hopes the F.A. may have had of letting snoring canines lie. Of course he had paid his players – how else was he going to build up a side to beat teams like Blackburn Rovers? – he not unreasonably asked.

The rest of that year, 1884, saw the lining up of three schools of thought – the amateurs, pure and simple, who believed that money was an evil that had to be cast from their midst before it tainted the whole game; the amateurs who did not wish to see professionalism but were wise enough to see its inevitability and decided that it should be admitted but strictly controlled; and a small percentage of Northerners who were prepared for a free-for-all in wages and transfers. To complicate the issue, many of the first group joined the second group in the following eighteen months, and the lobbying that went on must have been as frantic and exciting as a goal-mouth scramble.

On February 11th, a proposal of C. W. Alcock's that the time had come to legalise professionalism was discussed at a sub-committee, where it was opposed by an amendment from the die-hards that the time had *not* come. On the 28th, the issue reached a General Meeting. Alcock repeated his proposal with the addendum that a Special General Meeting should be called to work out the details if the principle was carried. It was countered by an amendment from N. Lane 'Pa' Jackson (one of those who had changed sides in the intervening fortnight and whose stand against the introduction of people 'in the game for what they could make out of it' has to be weighed against the fact that he himself did very well out of his own writings on the game). His amendment, strongly supported by J. C. Clegg of Sheffield (a dry, blunt and domineering man of whom it was later said that 'to oppose him was unwise') stated 'This meeting considers that the existence of veiled professionalism, and the importation of players are serious evils calling for prompt legislation ...' Note the use of the word 'evils' with its moral implication.

Off to another sub-committee went the issue or issues for further examination. Meanwhile, the Scottish Football Association, somewhat tired of seeing their star players disappearing over the border like rabbits vanishing down a rabbit-hole, made their opinion crystal clear that professionalism should be ruthlessly crushed. And in 1885, they duly banned 68 Scots players who had gone to play in England.

The sub-committee reported in June 1884 to a Special General Meeting. Their solution, a host of regulations with the uneasy whiff of a witch-hunt about them, was contained in a circular that went out in early October. Within a week, the document had provoked special meetings in Lancashire, at Blackburn and Manchester, of aggrieved clubs who saw from its clauses that in return for being allowed to pay one day's wages for time lost, their imported players would be banned from the F.A. Cup. Unsurprisingly, the threat of large scale secessions from the Football Association loomed.

This created, in its turn, something of a panic at headquarters, and that English panacea for all ills, the sub-committee, was again resorted to. Alcock again proposed, and this time, N. Lane Jackson brought himself to second, a motion 'to legalize professionalism under stringent conditions'. Surviving the sub-committee on a 7–4 vote and a full Association committee on a 13–5 vote, the motion reached another Special General Meeting in January 1885. Here it scraped home by a whisker of delegate votes 113–108, which, maddeningly enough, was not the two-thirds majority necessary to substantiate its implementation. Another General Meeting in March brought a stronger vote in favour, 106–69, but still not a two-thirds majority, and a further rigmarole of a sub-committee and a formal questionnaire had to be gone through before a July 1885 Special General Meeting with only fifty present (the ones who stayed away could be forgiven for thinking there could be nothing fresh to say on the issue) divided 35–15, a necessary two-thirds, in favour of professionalism 'under stringent conditions'. (The 'conditions' were a host of residential and registration requirements.)

Therefore, from 1885 onwards, the governing authority of the game was largely composed of men with public school and aristocratic backgrounds, dedicated to amateurism as a desirable ideal, but prepared to tolerate the professionals who would otherwise have broken away, providing that they themselves could control the new trend. Over succeeding years they were caught in the middle of the crossfire between two warring forces. On their left was the professional group who wanted the authority to reflect the increasing power of the North and for whom that authority did not move half fast enough. On their right, were the diehard amateurs who felt any concession was bad, and were determined, if possible, to ensure that no more were made. The latter group said they were preventing the game from being ruined – they meant from being ruined for *them*, passé as the Old Boy teams had become against the strength of professional teams.

Three years of constitutional wrangles, coup d'etats, resignations and resolutions followed (including the setting up of an International Board and F.A. Council). And in 1888, a powerful new kingdom grew up within the F.A. empire. This was the Football League.

Its formation, originating in a letter sent by William McGregor of Aston Villa to a number of professional clubs, stemmed from the same sort of economic considerations that a factory owner would apply to his business – that it was inefficient to have a valuable plant standing idle. Equally, it was silly to pay wages to star players and have them standing idle on a Saturday afternoon because of the casual state of the average fixture list. Most lists comprised Cup matches (and, if one was unlucky, a quick exit from the knock-out competition after one or two matches) and a leavening of occasional 'friendly' fixtures. The solution to the problem was obviously a league of clubs to play each other on a home and away basis whereby the club was ensured a supply of opposition, and its supporters a regular and more predictable entertainment.

Two meetings followed on the sending of McGregor's letter, and professional league football, subsequently the life-blood of the game, was born. For teams like Aston Villa who had bored their spectators with twenty to nil victories against inferior cup opposition (there were no exemptions in early rounds then and George Copley, the Aston Villa goalkeeper, had spent one tedious slaughter sitting on a chair thoughtfully provided for him in his goalmouth) the League was a god-send. No one, however, even McGregor, who wrote in 1906 'I did not foresee that it would sweep everything before it in the way it has', could have anticipated what an impact the new League would have.

McGregor was equally honest about the intentions of the new monster in the F.A. midst:

By the very nature of things the League must be a selfish body. Its interests are wholly bound up in the welfare of its affiliated clubs, and what happens outside is, in a sense, of a secondary importance only.

Therefore, from as early as 1888, it is possible to see the potential friction which continues today. One body has responsibility for all kinds of football from international matches to boys' clubs and schools, while another exists within it for whom the interest of the professional league club must be paramount. And so, in the 1970s, when top players can be caught in the squabbles between the conflicting interests of the club engaged in a crucial domestic league or European cup battle, and the country qualifying for a world or European competition, an administrative formula constructed to answer the quite different conditions in the 1880's still has to be applied.

League and Association officials are often criticised for their narrow-sighted approach to one another's problems. Sometimes, the criticisms are just, but in fairness is it not true that an administrative pattern set up in 1888 to answer the demands of 1888 can hardly be expected to continue to serve its purpose ninety years on? And unless a new structure is devised adequately to reflect the march of time in those ninety years, mortal men are being asked to perform duties that would tax a coachload of saints. How long, one wonders, it is to be before we have the courage to demolish the administrative house, and build one more fitting to contemporary needs?

To return to the past, Alcock's *Football Annual* for 1890 makes it quite clear as to what priority he gave to the new League, and what sort of interest there was among his southern readers. The League gets one page with the final table and one paragraph of copy, doings in the provincial associations get 27 pages, and the public school elevens and fifteens get 21 pages of descriptive matter and nine pages of results.

The annual also says, shades of things to come, that:

The interest in Inter-Association matches has been considerably discounted in the Northern districts by the increasing importance of inter-club contests. The strictly business-like spirit in which the League is conducted has prevented the clubs . . . from rendering the same amount of assistance to their District Associations as in the past . . .

and made it quite clear that this was a Bad Thing;

> The importance attached to meetings between clubs under certain conditions is not without its advantages, but if carried to excess, as it undoubtedly is in many parts, is calculated to do harm to, rather than benefit the game . . .

And as the south raised its eyebrows, and often its arms in horror, the northern supporters liked what they saw and continued to support it in ever increasing numbers. They did not leave written testimony of their support for professional football, but, more importantly, they went to see it throughout the 1890's and ever since.

To the south, and particularly to middle-class Philistine opinion for whom respectability was all, an amalgam of arrogance, snobbery and moral reproof was the best they could muster. Two magazine articles (originally traced by Morris Marples for his scholarly *History of Football*) demonstrate the trend. In *The Nineteenth Century* for October 1892, an article 'The New Football Mania' by Charles Edwardes thought

> The new football is a far more effectual arouser of the unregenerate passions of mankind than either a political gathering or a race meeting . . .

and a football ground was not a place a gentleman would frequent, for on the terrace

> . . . your neighbour uses language not to be found in grammars for the use of schools . . . (and) . . . of drinking, it may be taken for granted that there is abundance

and in case anyone missed the point, he emphasised

> The multitude flock to the field in their workaday dirt, and with their workaday adjectives very loose on their tongues . . .

Matters had not improved six years later when the cry was

taken up by Ernest Ensor in the *Contemporary Review* for November 1898. This time the title was 'The Football Madness' but what Mr Ensor lacked in originality, he made up in venom. For him, the way football had been adopted in the north was part of the trouble;

> There it was passionately adopted by that people whose warped sporting instincts are so difficult to understand* ...

Professional players had been imported when 'the warped instincts asserted themselves' for 'the worst feature of professional football is its sordid nature'.

Warming to the theme, he lashed out in all directions – the professional footballer 'is an idler'. Having given a wholly partial view of the split in rugby between union and league where 'the possession of money has sapped the morals of clubs in Yorkshire and Lancashire' and 'petty treachery, mean cheating and espionage' was rife, he turned back to soccer. He thundered

> Association has touched pitch and been shockingly defiled ... the effect of League matches and cup ties is thoroughly evil ... the system is bad for the players, worse for the spectators. The former learn improvident habits, become vastly conceited, whilst failing to see that they are treated like chattels, and cannot help but be brutalised. The latter are injured physically and morally ...

Meanwhile, the majority of the sporting public shrugged off the moral dangers they were so dangerously skirting and turned up to Cup and League matches regardless.

In 1891, Blackburn Rovers again came out top of the heap in the Cup Final at the Oval. Cup entries had gone up to 161, and the Final crowd to 23,000. Blackburn, curiously enough, played their final opponents, Notts County, in the league a week before the Oval match and lost 7–1 but any punters who took this as an omen were doomed to disappointment for Rovers upended form in a 3–1 win. It was a day of glory for their older players for not only did Townley add another goal to the three he had scored in the 1890 final, but James Forrest, their

---

*He means Northerners *en masse* and says blandly 'Humour is not a general gift in the North'(!)

half-back, got his fifth Cup winners medal – a record it is difficult to see anyone equalling, let alone exceed.*

Next year, it was an all-Birmingham final and the use of the Oval for the last time due to protests from the Surrey CCC who had to use the ground after it had been cut up by football studs. Before the match took place, West Bromwich Albion were given so little chance of beating their mighty rivals Aston Villa that it was suggested in Birmingham that the Albion withdraw and concede the match to save themselves from disgrace and what seemed the entire Birmingham population from paying out rail fares. They did not concede and with Villa's beefy forward line played off the park by the Albion half-back line of Reynolds, Perry and Groves, they won in a canter 3–0. Searching desperately for excuses and a bit of therapy by destruction, Villa supporters returned home and smashed goalkeeper Warner's windows. Warner was, said an early football writer, 'very badly treated by members of the lower orders in Birmingham'.

With the demise of the Oval as a Cup Final venue, attention shifted to Fallowfield, Manchester in 1893 where 45,000 people, some off and some on the field, saw the favourites Everton beaten under protest by Wolverhampton Wanderers 1–0. (Lord Kinnaird, the only man present able to uphold the protest about pitch encroachment, had already left the ground.) The goal was scored by the Wolves captain Allen with a shot from half-way that soared like a 6 iron golf shot over the head of an Everton goalkeeper with the sun in his eyes.

The Wolves supporters, before and after the match, showed all the modern manifestations of fan-worship. They circulated sheet music of a song about their team, wore black and gold rosettes (to this even Lord Dartmouth is believed to have succumbed) and built a street in their city called Fallowfield Terrace where every gatepost was adorned with a stone replica of the cup and every house named after a player, all in memory of the great day the Cup came to Wolverhampton.

The crowd excesses of 1893 meant Everton's own ground

*A player the Rovers signed five years later, Bob Crompton who won 42 English caps at right back from 1902–14, a cultured and fleet-footed player, never got a Cup winner's medal at all and in that, he was more representative of most players than Forrest – one reason why the medal is still valued so highly.

was tried in 1894. There 37,000 people saw Notts County, helped by centre forward Logan's hat-trick, demolish an illness-stricken Bolton 4–1, but no one seemed very happy at the choice, for it was Crystal Palace that was tried in 1895, and that was where the final remained until the outbreak of the First World War.

The first at the Palace was the last at the Oval replayed – Aston Villa and West Bromwich Albion. West Brom had the great W. I. Bassett on their right wing, a fleet-footed 5 ft 5 in player who could stop dead when flat out, and specialised in pushing the ball past a full back and running around him outside the touchline. He and his inside-right Roddy McLeod built a fine understanding but it did them no good that day. This time Villa supporters could live with themselves and their WBA neighbours on the strength of a 1–0 win. The goal itself came within 30 seconds of the kick-off and was missed by hundreds of latecomers – not that this stopped those who missed it describing it when they got back home. All the Villa club could do was to describe the Cup to their supporters, for they got it back to Birmingham, put it on display in the window of a boot and shoe shop, and lost it to a burglar. Whether the thief was for Villa or Albion, history, alas, does not tell us.

The *Football Annual* of 1895 had comforting words for those disturbed by football's growth. Making a clear about-turn from its 1890 issue, it now thought that 'the game has not suffered in any way in its general tone' because of professionalism. In fact,

> The professional teams mostly play the game in a sports-manlike way, which some of the professedly amateur teams might do well to imitate.

Not able to beat them, some at least of the amateur spokesmen had decided to join them.

Entries and crowds for the Cup continued to swell. 210 clubs entered for 1896 and 48,836 people saw Spiksley, Sheffield Wednesday's outside left, score both goals in a 2–1 win over Wolves, who had changed the black and gold quarters worn to victory in 1893 for natty stripes, an omen that their captain Harry Wood who had played three years previously must have regretted.

The following year, the entries were up to 244 and the 65,891 crowd were treated to one of the classic finals of the series. Aston Villa were back riding high on a crest of success that had brought them the Football League Championship by an unprecedented eleven clear points. Determined to stop them achieving the 'Double' was Everton.

Villa are worth closer study, for their prowess from about 1892 to 1900 made them the most glamorous team in the land. Their growth to fame and fortune was a familiar pattern. Since their humble beginnings in 1874 as youths belonging to the Aston Villa Wesleyan Chapel, their footballing gospel spread as fast and as powerfully as had the doctrines of Wesley himself in an earlier age. They had in Fred Rinder an administrator prepared to brook no nonsense – he had led a club *coup d'etat* in 1892 when he and his supporters brought charges of maladministration against the committee, became secretary of a new committee himself and by the introduction of turnstiles reaped in for the club £250 a match. The previous takings had been about £75 and it was suspected, probably correctly, that the difference between the two sums could be explained by the depth of the old gatemen's pockets.

The new income was used wisely and well. Captain and inside-right John Devey (unlucky in internationals because he had to compete for the England berth with Steve Bloomer), was thought old when he joined Villa in 1891 but only relinquished the captaincy in 1901 with five League championship medals and two Cup winners medals. Under him, the club amassed some talented players. From WBA, they got Reynolds, the half back who had helped to ruin their Cup hopes in 1892. At centre half they had the inimitable granite-faced Scot James Cowan, and no lumbering giant he, for he walked off with the Powderhall sprint in 1896. (Villa themselves were none too pleased at this particular piece of athleticism as it took place during his absence from training because of 'a weak back'!) His affability was said to increase in direct proportion to his alcoholic intake, but even in his cups, to interrupt his singing of mournful Scottish ballads was to court disaster. Devey's protegé Charlie Athersmith was on the right wing alongside his mentor, and John Campbell was the centre forward ready to capitalise on the gaps these two opened up in a defence. In their backs, the halves Reynolds,

Cowan and the ball-playing Crabtree could switch from attack to defence with bewildering speed.

Now at the Palace on April 10th 1897 Everton had quite a task before them. They failed, but in the failing, they covered themselves in glory too, particularly their seemingly inexhaustible inside right Bell. The game was played at a furious but controlled pace but was decided, though none knew it then, in the last thirty minutes before the interval. A classic burst of short passing between Athersmith and Devey was crowned by a scoring shot from Cambell. 1–0. That was merely a signal for Bell to redouble his efforts and he equalised with a solo run five minutes later. Second blood to Everton and shortly afterwards third blood also when Boyle* scored from a free kick. 1–2. Ten minutes later, Crabtree took a free kick and Wheldon made it 2–2. Just before the teams could take a break with the spoils evenly divided, Villa scored what was to prove the winner. Reynolds crossed the ball from a corner and the ubiquitous Crabtree** ran in to head it home. 3–2 it was and 3–2 it remained although there was 45 minutes of football, suspense and panic left to go through before the final whistle.

The 1897 Cup win, with the added lustre of being the second leg of the 'Double', reminds us that Villa, founder members of the League, had been a force in league football for some time. The Villa feat of 1897 was repeating the double first performed by Preston North End in 1889 who had followed it in 1890 with the Championship alone.

Under John Goodall, Preston were very much a 'manufactured' team of three Lancashire men joined by an errant Welshman and seven Scots – from its inception therefore, League success came to those who worked, prepared and bought for it. The reign of Preston was halted by the brief but glorious flowering of Sunderland's 'team of all the talents'. Aided by Hugh Wilson, a Scottish right back who could throw the ball in some fifty yards (one-handed, which was not yet illegal),

---

*In the *Times* on the following Monday and repeated in Tony Pawson's *100 Years of the FA Cup*, these goals are credited to Holt (1) and Devey (2)– I have relied on Peter Morris' *Aston Villa* for, I hope, a more accurate account coming as it does from Birmingham sources. It is worth remembering shirts were not numbered until the thirties.
**ibid.

Sunderland from 1892–1895 won the League three times and were runners-up once.

Then came Villa who from 1894–1900 were Champions five times (1894, 1896, 1897, 1899 and 1900) in addition to the Cup successes we have already seen. In 1899, they won in climactic fashion, after slipping down the table to sixth in 1897–8 as their double team crumbled. All depended on the final game at Villa Park against Liverpool, who lay second and wanted the two points to win the title themselves. With the trophy on view in the stand ready for the victors to pick up, Villa destroyed Liverpool in a first half of magic which left them 5–0 in the lead. After that the second half was a mere formality. And, before the fire had died down, they were champions again in 1900 with a new record total for the league of fifty points.

Villa were among the fittest sides in the country, but that did not mean much for there was neither today's training schedules to fulfil nor today's heavy fixture list. West Brom's Bassett has left us a picture of what the average professional did in the way of training. A typical day would be a six-mile *walk* (great store was placed in the value of walking for all sportsmen) at not too demanding a pace, plus a work-out with Indian clubs, or a few laps around the ground 'according to the amount each required'. Some added short sprints too but of this Bassett disapproved – 'there is always a danger of overdoing this kind of training. Men who indulge in it much are liable to sudden breakdowns . . . I never used to do sprinting practice'. This, apart from the obligatory bath (usually cold) and a rub down, was it, except that the players were allowed ball practice once a week as a special treat.*

It is safe therefore to presume that most Edwardian successes at sport were based not on acquired fitness and skill but on pure undeveloped talent. That goes a long way to explain how many double internationals and all round sportsmen there were – even at the highest levels, men could still get by on talent alone.

Even on the talented Villa, fortune did not always smile.

*The lightness of preparation was not untypical. A journalist who visited the Tottenham Hotspur club headquarters in 1904 called them 'the lightest trained team in existence' and recorded that the players spent far more time at the billiards and chess tables provided by the club than they did at football training.

Worth recording for the light it casts on the sometimes ludicrous decisions made by officialdom, was a match played by them at Sheffield Wednesday in November 1898. With Villa losing 1–3, the match was abandoned after 79½ minutes because of the descending gloom. The following March (1899) the club was ordered to Sheffield to play the remaining 10½ minutes! Unsurprisingly, Sheffield scored another and the match, technically lasting four months, finished 1–4.

A year earlier, they hit more serious inconvenience at the hands of the game's administrators. Having sold their goalkeeper Whitehouse to Newton Heath, they signed a new player to replace him in Billy George. As a result of an enquiry made into the affair, the club was fined £50 for illegalities and George himself, Rinder and Ramsay, their secretary, were all suspended for a month. This incident was paralleled elsewhere during the nineties.

Transfers were a major source of irritation between the Football League and the Football Association, as were a number of financial questions arising out of the growth of league football. Villa, for example, in the 1888–9 season took £1,042 at league matches alone (£849 of which found its way to the players) and by 1904–5, they were taking over £13,000 (less generously, because of a restricted wage policy, only about £5,000 of this went to the players). In 1904–5, there were profits to be had for clubs. Newcastle United had the highest profits at £5,487 but about half a dozen clubs cleared over £5,000 for the season. At the other end of the scale, clubs had losses of £500 and more, with the once mighty Blackburn Rovers losing the most (£1,542). I give these figures because they contrast very nicely with Aston Villa's first recorded gate of 5s 3d in 1874, and because they give us an economic background to events.

If we recall the proliferation of meetings in 1885 described earlier, it will be remembered that the FA had eventually agreed to allow professionalism 'under stringent conditions'. The incorporation of the new Football League into the parent body three years later brought new men into the administration of the game and shifted some of the balance of power. These new men, spokesmen for the League clubs, got the 'stringent conditions' abolished by 1889. Piqued by the turn about, Major Marindin the President of the FA resigned to be replaced by

Lord Kinnaird, while the new Chairman of the FA Council was the domineering J. C. Clegg, whose power and influence had been growing and who was determined to stamp out abuses when and where he saw them. Transfers and professionalism generally were considered by him to be abuses. (Antipathy to Clegg was supposed to have contributed to Marindin's resignation).

By 1891, the FA had a professional clerk in charge of the registration of professional players, but what happened if a player wanted to leave one club and play for another? There were two views – the FA thought that any contract between player and club should cease at the end of the season, but the League, of course, took the view that the club still had rights over its players even when the year was up.

Some idea of the way men could pore over the small print of regulations to find loopholes may be gathered by the fact that the FA passed a rule in 1892 to forbid barristers and solicitors from pleading a club's or a player's cause unless they were serving in a dual capacity as club secretary.

At the end of 1893, what the players should receive for their services was fiercely debated at a General Meeting of the Football League. Four specific proposals were put to the meeting:

1. That no player should get more than £140 per annum with the option of a maximum of £1 a week in the summer. 2. That a £10 signing-on fee should be payable but *only* to non-League players, and that any transfer fee from club to club should be decided by the Management Committee (!). 3. All payments should be entered in the books which the League could inspect at any time. 4. Any infringements could render the offending club liable to a £200 fine, a deduction of six league points or expulsion without the right of appeal.

This pious package got a 16–16 vote on the first clause, failed for the lack of a two-thirds majority, and the other three clauses were hurriedly withdrawn. The deal had been sabotaged by the big clubs who saw it as a threat to their capacity to pay what they liked to attract players, and who wished to continue to poach any talent, League or non-league that was around.

(By 1893, professionalism had begun to spread beyond its original areas, for in that year Scotland belatedly legalised it, and in the South, there were enough professional teams to justify the formation of the Southern League in 1894.)

In February 1894, the FA stepped in where the League had failed to tread and a proposal by J. C. Clegg was carried. Among other demands, its fourth clause was adamant – no club was allowed to receive or pay a sum of money for the transfer of a player. This was the official attitude but there is much evidence to suggest that the ruling was frequently evaded, ignored or paid lip service alone. The evaders who were caught – Aston Villa were accused of poaching when they acquired Crabtree from Burnley in 1895, for example, for £300 and the receipts of a Villa v Burnley match – probably represented the visible tip of a very large iceberg.

The authority of the League itself was constantly undermined by the attitudes of the more powerful in their midst. Rulings would be issued, and then, when they became inconvenient to follow, were changed into the toothless 'requests', culminating in the ultimate absurdity of November 1895 when the League Management Committee 'advised' its players not to challenge referee's rulings on the field!

J. C. Clegg was also the mastermind behind the memorandum issued by the FA at the end of 1899. An informal meeting between FA and FL representatives in March, at which, predictably, William McGregor had defended transfers and Clegg and Alcock opposed them, produced a circular attempting to end transfers but recognising that clubs were entitled to be reimbursed if they sold players who had already commanded fees. Clegg now followed this circular with the latest memorandum which stated that attempts by clubs to interfere with a player's right to leave at the end of the season, or demands for a sum for his release, were both contrary to FA Rules. Buying and selling of players was in every way 'unsportsmanlike' and 'most objectionable'. Furthermore, the rumoured practice of lowly clubs grooming young players and then selling them, was, 'applied to human beings, altogether discreditable'.

Despite the opposition of the League, the document again recommended that unless a club was being honestly reimbursed for expenses incurred no more than £10 should be paid.

As the League increasingly assumed the role of an employers' association, and, like most similar organisations of the period, one which could be selfish and reactionary, the FA chose to be the kindly paternal overseer, but like most fathers, it would try to crack down hard when it felt the rod could no longer be spared. By 1900, the FA had 8,000 odd clubs in its charge – small wonder that it often found the brood unruly. Wearily, the FA for the moment, continued to shoulder their responsibilities.

The financial affairs of professional clubs continued to fill Association agendas, and the 1900 annual meeting produced and passed a resolution that the maximum wage of professional footballers was to be £4 a week. The decision, made as it was in the interests of small clubs who could afford to pay no more than the £4, if that, was hotly contested then and at the next annual meeting in 1901. In 1901, the big clubs, notably Aston Villa and Liverpool, got a majority for an amendment allowing them to pay more if they so desired, but as the majority was not of the magical two-thirds variety, the amendment failed. Instead, the FA Rules officially incorporated (Rule 32 of May 1901) £208 as a maximum wage for footballers. Any additional bonuses for winning matches were specifically disallowed. For the next few years, attempts by wealthy clubs to get the rule changed were legion, but such an economic absurdity was to stand for many decades.

But if the FA were committed officially to shouldering the burden, behind the committee room doors they were less happy about it. Their official historian, Geoffrey Green, has revealed that in 1904, the FA took the line of least resistance, and handed over control of club finances to the League. But, presumably in case anyone thought that they were abdicating part of their powers, they did not even minute so major a decision in their records. Only six years later, in April 1910, were all financial references, with the exception of the £208 maximum wage, expunged from FA Rules.

This secret and silent abdication must have lead to some heart-searching shortly afterwards for barely had the action been taken, when the Alf Common affair hit the 1905 headlines. Middlesbrough, lingering perilously at the foot of Division 1, paid £1,000 to Sunderland for Common. (For the expense, Middlesbrough soon had the satisfaction of their first away win in two years.) That a four-figure sum could change hands for a footballer's services was looked on by some as despicable, unworthy and downright immoral. And if rules meant anything at all, it was also illegal.

Putting the best possible face on it, the FA neither took action against the player or the clubs concerned but passed the buck to the Rules Revision Committee who, in a classic case of bolting the stable door after the horse had gone, recommended that after January 1st, 1908, no transfer fee should exceed £350. The rule duly came into effect on that date but by then it was open to many abuses. (For example, what was to stop a club paying £350 to another for a star player, and making up a higher fee by taking half a dozen players with two left feet along with him at £350 each to make up a more realistic fee?) Having been three years in the making, the rule had to be withdrawn after a bare three months in execution. Perhaps the best comment on the whole affair was a contemporary cartoon in which Common stood with a £1,000 price ticket on him, while a seductive Grecian lady marked Middlesbrough slid a shapely arm around his waist, and held out the other to fend off a grotesque figure looming in the background as 'the Ghost of the Second Division'.

Coming not singly but in battalions, troubles continued to batter away at the door of FA headquarters. First came approaches from professional players who gradually, if timorously, saw that their own interests could easily be forgotten in the power struggles at the top. An attempt to form a Players Union had been made in October 1893 by a Wolverhampton Wanderers goalkeeper, but his pioneering spirit had foundered on the apathy of his fellow players, particularly when the attempt made by poorer clubs in the Football League in that year to limit wages to £140 per annum had failed to receive the necessary majority.

A National Union of Association Players flowered briefly in 1899 but that too died a sudden death. By 1907, however, there was more serious support from players who belatedly saw that if they did not speak up for themselves, there were others who would speak for them, and not necessarily to their advantage. In December 1907, a Football Players' and Trainers' Union was formed.

For the moment, brotherly solidarity was all, and the happy band was accorded a fatherly welcome from the FA. In March 1908, the FA Council gave its consent (late again!) to the union's formation, and promised support for a fund-raising fixture between Manchester United and Newcastle United; but, just in case the new group ever got ideas above its station, reserved the right to inspect the Union's annual balance sheet.

The benevolent paternalism did not last long. In 1909, the union affiliated to the Federation of Trade Unions and then the balloon went up. Immediately, the FA and the FL who, as we have seen, had not been exactly bosom buddies over the years, closed ranks in the face of the common enemy. No one actually said that the national game was threatened by creeping socialism, but the inference was there. And in illuminating contrast to the shifting compromises made when the culprits breaking FA rules were powerful clubs, Dad now turned very nasty.

Strongly supported by the Football League (for when did any Edwardian employers' association look warmly upon unionists?), the Football Association, with, we may be sure, Clegg as prime mover, withdrew FA recognition of the Union, ordered all its members to resign from the union forthwith and suspended the Union Secretary and Chairman from football management. Prepared to tolerate a toy poodle, they were not prepared to keep a bulldog in case it bit.

The gloss placed on this witch-hunt was that a Union federated to other unions outside football might bring games to a standstill in sympathetic strikes. This danger, if it ever really existed outside the imaginations of the FA officials, must have been minimal – if any industrial striker had been asked, he would surely have preferred ninety minutes of football to relieve the tedium of a strikebound week to any insignificant support the footballers' union could have given him.

Despite the militancy of a few players, some of whom held out without pay for fourteen weeks, the League made contingency lists of amateur players who could be called on to fulfill the League fixtures and the strike collapsed in disorder. The Union called off the strike, withdrew from the Federation of Trades Unions and recognised the ultimate authority of the FA. It had proved a toy poodle after all. And it took another forty years before it had the courage to try to bite again – which is why it was only in 1961 that the absurdity of a maximum wage was finally abolished. And why, in Brian Glanville's memorable words*, it was possible for

*Soccer: a Panorama, p. 29.

... the unbroken spirit of the Victorian ironmasters actually to *reduce* the exiguous maximum wage of a League professional from £9 to £8 a week, soon after the First World War.

The Players Union got another bloody nose in 1912 when they backed Kingaby of Aston Villa in a test-case brought against the club (who were backed in their turn by the Football League). The player alleged that the high transfer fee fixed by the club was losing him his chance of employment elsewhere. On a defence submission, the jury was dismissed and the decision given by the judge was that his contract with Villa was legally binding, and costs were awarded to Villa. As was usual for the period, the law was on the employer's side.

When it had come to the crunch, the FA had had no serious trouble in putting down incipient professional rebellion in their ranks. However, when it came to the amateurs and their spokesmen at headquarters and elsewhere, all was by no means sweetness and light.

Much of the ensuing conflict in the period stemmed from the quite different attitudes towards football taken by the public school men on the one hand, and by other men for whom J. J. Bentley, a prominent official of both League and Association, spoke when he said

It is all very well ... to say that a man should play for the pure love of the game. Perhaps he ought, but to the working man it is simply impossible.

Resentment built up in the amateur ranks as the game which they had in essence invented was taken away from them by its new exponents. Not only had their chances of competing on level terms with professionals in the Cup and in the International team dwindled, but the game itself was changing as it encompassed its new adherents.

The first point of friction of our period was over the 1891 legislation. This sensibly pre-empted at least some of the weekly disputes about matches by making goal-nets compulsory. It also added to the laws of the game, and it was this which stuck in many an amateur throat, the provision of a penalty kick. Then, as today, the penalty was to be awarded for an *intentional* offence in the penalty area. The public school men argued that any offence in the area by their players was *bound* to be accidental, and to award a penalty kick would be to besmirch the honour of the culprit and to cast the aspersion that a man's sense of fair play and honourable conduct had temporarily deserted him.

I think this attitude is extremely important and self-revealing for it shows the Edwardian public school man at his best and at his weakest simultaneously. To his eternal credit is the fact that for the duration of a football game, he was prepared to place the importance of self and of victory below the priority of conforming to a self-imposed ethical and moral standard. In essence, it shows him as a follower of the rule of law without which there can be no useful civilisation. But, and it is a big but, it also shows him to be quite incapable of looking beyond his own insular orbit, and moreover, represents an expectancy that the world at large will conform to his narrow and distorted picture of it. Despite its modest façade, it is the highest of arrogances. From such a stance came the anti-intellectual, anti-scientific, anti-art, anti-European, anti-American, anti-world and ultimately anti-life, attitudes that may well have doomed Edwardian England even if the First World War had never happened.

In football in the three year old League, there was need of a penalty as indeed there still is. As more store was placed upon winning as well as playing, and men being men, there were abuses, rough play and many an unseemly scene on football grounds. Referees were abused, and occasionally pelted and attacked. Some matches ended in utter confusion. One fixture between Burnley and Blackburn (at which incidentally Clegg was the referee) came to an absolute *impasse* when ten of the Blackburn players walked off in protest against a decision, and the one man remaining refused to take the inevitable free kick for offside. Yet it is possible now to see such matters in perspective as the inevitable birth pangs and teething troubles of a strong infant who became more ruly as time went on. What is really remarkable is that the standards of sportmanship remained as high as they did, and that abuses were more marked by their absence than their presence.

The morality of the penalty did continue to cause controversy. In 1902, the FA had to reprimand the amateur Old Boy teams

The sporting Prince of
Wales – Edward, later King
Edward VII, participates in
a game of lawn tennis at
Baden Baden with a
decorative doubles partner

Monarch and racehorse
owner – King Edward VII
accompanied by the Prince
of Wales (later King
George V) attends the 1909
Derby, looking pleased
with life and the result

A gallery of Edwardian football greats – from left to right, Athersmith (Aston Villa), Bambridge (Swifts), Foulke (Sheffield United), Bloomer (Derby County), Goodall (Preston and Derby), G. O. Smith (Corinthians), Needham (Sheffield United), Spiksley (Sheffield Wednesday), Bassett (West Bromwich Albion). They all played for England

Left: C. W. Alcock, a powerful Edwardian administrator, a J.P. who was Secretary of the Football Association, Secretary of the Surrey County Cricket Club, and editor of both the *Football Annual* and *Cricket* magazine. *Right:* With his toothpick firmly in place, Billy Meredith demonstrates his technique for centres. Meredith, football and controversy became inseparable in the era

Despite the mid-air ballet, Southampton failed to score one goal in this 1900 Cup Final at Crystal Palace. The first Southern team to play a Final for seventeen years, they went down 4–0 to Bury

One of the best Edwardian Cup Finals – S. T. Dadd's impression of some of the action between Tottenham Hotspur and Sheffield United in the 1901 Final. Tottenham won but only after a replay

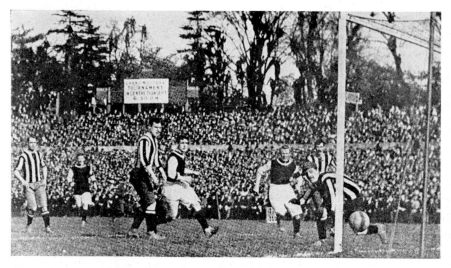

Harry Hampton of Aston Villa (fourth from right) scores the first of his two goals against Newcastle in the 1905 Final – the start of an uncanny hoodoo that Crystal Palace had for Newcastle

Newcastle United back at the Palace for the 1911 Cup Final. Despite the overpopulation of the Bradford City half of the field in this picture, Bradford survived to win a replay

Freeman of Burnley scores almost from the penalty spot to defeat Liverpool in the 1914 Cup Final

A general view of Crystal Palace during the 1914 Cup Final. Among the 72,778 people was King George V, the first time a reigning monarch had attended a Cup Final

The 1891 battle for the Calcutta Cup. The series between England and Scotland (dark shirts) was interrupted by controversies off the field. England lost this match by three goals to one goal and their performance was described as 'the very worst display which any English team ever gave'

England score one of their four tries against Wales at Blackheath in 1892. The unsuccessful Welsh tackler is probably the great W. J. Bancroft of Swansea

The original All Blacks in action against Midland Counties at Leicester in 1905. Gallaher plays outside the scrum in a role his friends called a 'rover' and his enemies an 'obstructor'. In this picture, the latter is clearly more accurate

No prizes offered for spotting the line-out infringements from both the All Blacks and the Midland Counties – Gallaher, not in the picture, has probably thrown in from touch, a nice precedent for modern use of the hooker. Note that only the touring team wears numbers

entered in the new Arthur Dunn Cup for their refusal to recognise the penalty. Even after that, the attitude lingered on. In 1907, C. B. Fry, who had played as an amateur with Southampton as one of his many sporting activities, could still write

> It is a standing insult to sportsmen to have to play under a rule which assumes that players intend to trip, hack and push their opponents, and to behave like cads of the most unscrupulous kidney. I say that the lines marking the penalty area are a disgrace to the playing field of a public school.

Presumably the cads of the most unscrupulous kidney who played professional football were expected to grin and bear the insult.

To add to the amateurs' grumbling discontent over the penalty, there was the 1896 controversy over scratch teams. Broadly speaking, a scratch team was a kind of all stars eleven drawn together to play a specific fixture, usually in mid-week. On the surface this appeared a harmless phenomenon of interest to no one but the players and sponsors and anyone else who cared to come along and watch. When the FA passed a resolution on October 12th 1896, requiring to know in advance who were to compose the scratch elevens and on what basis the team had been organised, anguished cries from the amateurs rent the heavens. This 'dictatorship' by Big Brother FA was intolerable. Precisely the same voices which had been raised against professionalism were now prepared to defend the scratch team. One of the FA's own officials, N. Lane 'Pa' Jackson, went so far as to refuse to comply with the ruling, and when he failed to get it overturned at a meeting at the end of the year, he resigned from the FA in a fit of pique.

This and similar examples of moral rectitude could be more sympathetically regarded were it not for the fact that many of the scratch teams were prime examples not of amateurism but of shamateurism. A closer examination reveals the hypocrisy. The sponsor of the scratch team would approach a professional club, offering a fixture which had the attraction of star players and the added piquance of a gentlemen v players aspect, and get a guarantee from the club of either a fee or a share of the gate, or both. The earnings were then shared among the players and the sponsor. Consequently, an amateur player could go home with a larger sum than the professional who only got a wage. In other words a gentleman could play football for money, but remain an amateur on the dubious basis that unlike the professional he did not need it!

Not all the scratch teams were guilty of this sort of thing, but we have the word of A. N. Hornby (the famous Lancashire cricketer) that such double standards were common. In the 1893–94 season, he attacked the Corinthians particularly, for according to him, the flower of English amateur football asked larger guarantees, issued no balance sheet, and distributed lavish expenses to players surpassing a professional's wages. Corinthians, one might add, were managed by 'Pa' Jackson.

No account of Edwardian football would be quite complete without some mention of the Corinthians. They were formed in 1882 by Jackson primarily to give English international players more opportunity to familiarise themselves with one another's play than was possible at their annual mauling by Scotland. International players, that is, providing they were public school and university men. Certainly they had talent – twice, in 1894 and 1895, they contributed the entire England elevens against Wales – and were often well organised too. Basically, they were an anachronism but unquestionably the only amateur team of equivalent strength to the professional league clubs, a standard of which they gave ample evidence by beating Preston's 'Double' team in 1889 by 5–0, League champions Aston Villa 2–1 in 1900, and Cup holders Bury 10–3 in 1904.

From 1900 to 1914 they produced eighteen internationals but after 1907 they played no matches against professional clubs (we shall see why later). In G. O. Smith, a slender and intellectual centre-forward who made the England berth his own for as long as he wanted it, a man who could shoot without warning, or when a defence mindful of his reputation closed around him, could devastate them with a scoring pass, the Corinthians produced their greatest player. His mighty reputation is still with us.

Smith represented amateurism at its best. Amateurism at its worst produced the third and final squabble following those about penalty awards and scratch teams. Lingering resentments that the FA was ever mindful of its 300 professional clubs but neglectful of the other 7,700 who represented over 200,000 amateur footballers, flared up again over the question whether the County Associations should permit professional clubs to affiliate. An attempt by the FA Council in 1902 to pass a resolution that no club could be refused affiliation had failed but the issue was merely postponed.

When it came up again, the opposition was strictly regional. A whole series of meetings were held, resignations were made and rescinded, documents and letters passed to and fro, all of which it would be tedious to catalogue in detail. The essence of the matter was that whatever happened elsewhere in the country, the Surrey and Middlesex Associations flatly refused to allow professional clubs to affiliate to their bodies. Packed as these bodies were with Old Boy clubs, they were determined that no professional should be allowed to sully their game. Professional footballers might be admirable men for all they knew but they were making sure their daughter clubs were not allowed to marry one.

Old Boy clubs like the Old Carthusians and the Old Westminster FC withdrew from the London Football Association, which had shown itself dangerously liberal in being prepared to follow the FA rules and admit professionals, and a new rebel body came into being. This group, the Amateur Football Defence Federation, was originally formed in 1906 to continue the struggle within the FA, but in 1907, as the FA courageously stuck to its guns, it became the independent Amateur Football Association, and broke away from the parent body. With them went some of the universities, the Corinthians, the Old Etonians and a host of other clubs. For the next seven years, football was rent in twain.

Seen from the vantage point of our own age, this schism in football looks curiously like a dress rehearsal for two of the most savage struggles in the Edwardian political field. In the football split of 1907, in the constitutional crisis in the Lords arising from Lloyd George's Budget of 1909, and in the attempted suborning of Ulster in 1912, is it not just possible to detect a common thread? In each case one has a move by a Tory minority, in normal circumstances the firmest of believers in following the rules of law and order, attempting to change the law as it stood when its operation was proving personally inconvenient, and when the attempt failed, taking the law into its own hands. One would not make any major claims for the validity of the parallel, but it is an interesting thought.

The Football Association received some welcome support on their stand and continued to be recognised as *the* authority for amateur football in most of the quarters which mattered. The international football body FIFA refused to recognise the rebel AFA as did the home country associations and those of Austria, Hungary, Germany, France, Belgium and the Netherlands among others. And despite attempted obstruction from the Hockey Association and the Rugby Football Union, both bastions of the so-called amateur spirit, it was the Football Association who were represented on and organised for, the British Olympic Association, then engaged in preparations for the 1908 Olympic Games to be held in London.

Nevertheless, they were also pilloried, particularly in the organs of the press which catered for the public school sportsman or for Philistine opinion. *Punch* in December 1908, carried an unpleasant article by, of all people, A. A. Milne, headed 'Football, Limited'. (This was a common sneer at the Football Association due to their incorporation as a limited company in 1903 under the Joint Stock Companies Act. Easily made to appear as if it were a case of a profit-making combine annexing greater power, the real reason was a far more innocent one. Shocked by the implications of the Ibrox disaster of 1902 when a stand collapsing at the Scotland v England match had killed 26 people and injured nearly 600, the FA had registered merely to avail themselves of the protection of limited liability.)

Milne dubbed FA headquarters 'the royal residence' ('a palace ... from which so many royal decrees and proclamations have been issued') and transformed FA officials, Clegg, Bentley, Pickford and Wall into Emperor Clegg, Lord Chief Justice Bentley, Archbishop Pickford and Marquis Wall. Clegg's autocratic methods were an obvious target, but his colleagues had done little to draw similar fire, and for Clegg himself it can be said that he was consistent and was only now applying to the die-hard amateurs the same treatment he had previously applied to professionals who had transgressed.

So, with ill-feeling on either side, seven long years passed before the FA and the AFA made up their differences. And then, after ticklish negotiations lasting from February 1912 till

February 1914, the rebels returned home to the parent body and football was thankfully restored to one overall authority.

The signing of the truce did not escape humorists' attention. According to W. Burton Baldry, the whole thing took place in song, a duet between the FA and the AFA. It went like this:

C. Wreford-Brown* (*sotto voce*)
I repent, and sink upon my knees,
To crave forgiveness, Mr Clegg
Take me back, and I'll work hard to please,
And never try to pull your leg,
I've been wrong, made blunders by the score,
And your indulgence I must beg.
I wont be a bad boy any more,
So try to love me, Mr Clegg!

J. C. Clegg (*through a megaphone*)
I am King! The FA is my throne,
O'er bags of gold I hold my sway,
Sir, how dare you call your soul your own,
And try to go your own sweet way?
Bring your men, let them be bought and sold
(And prices are not going down).
Come and hide your face within the fold,
For I forgive you, Wreford-Brown.

The duet, which appeared in *C. B. Fry's Magazine* in March 1914, bears so close a resemblance to the sentiments implicit in Milne's piece of seven years before, that we can be fairly sure that feelings had not cooled too much in the interim. As far back as April 1888, when the England international team travelled to Belfast to play against Ireland, the two amateurs in the team, Lindley and Walters had refused to travel on the same boat as the professionals, let alone share a hotel. Such prejudice would be a long time dying.

In these financial and administrative wrangles, we have strayed a long way from the field of play, but one hopes not without good reason for it is only against such a background that the full picture of Edwardian soccer can be seen. We left the Cup

*The Corinthian, Old Carthusian and England player and founder member of the rebel group.

with the classic Aston Villa v Everton final of 1897 and if contemporary accounts are to be believed, that was the high point of Cup football in the period. Even in 1914, writers were still saying that there had been no final to compare with it. For all that, there were some stirring struggles to come in the series.

Attendance (62,017) and entries (213) dropped for 1898, and there was slackening of public interest in the Nottingham Forest victory over Derby County by three goals to one. Its main interest now is that the Derby goal scorer was Steve Bloomer. This slight, pale-faced and lazy looking player was, according to one of his contemporaries 'a strange compound of the stoic and the philosopher', but he evidently had only to get the ball at his feet to give the lie to appearances, for then he became 'a man of action, a living force, a strong, relentless destroying angel'. His shooting prowess was feared and he had the quality, given only to the highest class of forward, of being able to hypnotise a goalkeeper like a stoat does a rabbit.

He was back at the Palace in the 1899 Final with Derby, but again the trophy eluded him and them. The menace of Bloomer was contained by the Sheffield United defence, and in particular by one of the greatest of Edwardian half-backs 'Nudger' Needham. (In league football there were few defenders of Needham's calibre and in a career lasting from 1892 to 1914, Bloomer, still playing at the ripe age of 40, scored 352 league goals). Needham played the ball so close to his feet he was always likely to get hurt, but in the big games for club or country, he was stout defender and constructive attacker by turn, doing it was said, the work of three ordinary players. His organisational talents brought United a 4–1 win. United's goalkeeper that day was Billy Foulke, a massive twenty odd stone Titan who could fill most of the space between the posts without moving a muscle. One Derby player, Macdonald, made the serious mistake of trying to charge Foulke into his own goal and rebounded some distance to general hilarity. That, and the courage of United's right back Thickett who played the game swathed in a fifty-yard bandage around two broken ribs, and downed a whole bottle of champagne at half-time to restore any lost calories, remained the highlights of the day.

The 1900 Final was very disappointing. Southampton, gallant

members of the Southern League and the first southern team to reach the final for 17 years, found Bury far too good for them and lost 4–0. That the spread of professionalism in the south was however bearing fruit is proved by the 1901 Final when London turned out in force and 110,820 people crammed into the ground, the trees, and the surrounding rooftops to see Tottenham Hotspur, another Southern League team, play Sheffield United. Tottenham had some difficulty in rising to the occasion and their forwards, often capable of dazzling inter-passing reminiscent of Preston and Aston Villa in previous years, were relatively ineffective. Needham was everywhere as usual, Foulke looked massive and impregnable in goal, and Sheffield scored first. But what Tottenham lacked in fluency they made up in determination and after 50 minutes they were 2–1 up. In the very next minute, Clawley the Tottenham goalkeeper fumbled the ball and Spurs' Bennett put it out of play. Up went the linesman's flag for a corner but to general amazement, the referee pointed to the centre spot, awarding a goal to Sheffield. He was the only man in the ground convinced the ball had crossed the Spurs' goal-line, but he was the one who mattered. 2–2 it was and 2–2 it remained at the end.

The replay was at Bolton and Spurs, who could have been forgiven for thinking the Gods were against them, again conceded an early goal but found some of their Southern League form to get three goals in the second half to take the Cup back to a London which had almost forgotten what it looked like.

Sheffield's turn came again in 1902, when they had to play both a Final and a replay against Southampton, drawing the Final 1–1 but clinching the rematch 2–1. This was also the first time the organisation of the Cup took its more familiar pattern of qualifying competitions and exemptions, culminating in 10 survivors and 22 exempted clubs playing off the remaining rounds – a sensible rationalisation of football's major competition.

The following year Derby, but not Bloomer who was injured, were back to play Bury. The Derby goalkeeper Fryer was overwhelmed by injury and general incompetence, and perhaps tedium at picking the ball out of the back of the net, for Bury scored six goals. Bury had the added satisfaction of winning the Cup without conceding a goal in any of the rounds.

It was a Lancashire fiesta in 1904 but Manchester City and Bolton, the finalists, failed to grip the imagination. Bolton incidentally got to the Final by beating Derby County 1–0 in the semi-final, leaving Derby with the unhappy record from 1896 to 1904 of losing four semi-finals and three Finals. In the Final itself, one goal was sufficient to win and it was scored by Manchester City's winger, Welshman Billy Meredith. Twenty minutes from the start, Meredith got the ball out of defence, in an offside position said many, the majority of them from Bolton, and dribbled on to score.

Meredith got 51 Welsh caps between 1895 and 1920, and but for the Great War would have had many more. His long, raking stride, his phenomenally accurate centres, his dark hair, and his sardonic air of controlling both ball and opponents without bothering to spit out the toothpick he kept between his strong teeth, brought him an adoring following, by no means all of it Celtic in origin, on every League ground in the country. Not a man to suffer fools or employers gladly, controversy and publicity often surrounded him in equal proportions.

A few months after the 1904 Final win, Manchester City were investigated by the FA for illegal transfer negotiations, most of the board were suspended, the team banned from playing and the club fined £500. This was bad enough but worse followed. A year later, Meredith was suspended for nearly three years for offering a bribe to an Aston Villa player to throw a league match. Meredith's defence was that he had been acting under the instructions of the club secretary! In March 1906, the FA were again investigating Meredith *at the request of the club.* Apparently, he had demanded wages from them while under suspension, but when the FA dug deeper, documents were produced to show that Meredith had been guaranteed compensation to shield the guilt of others. The sequel was that Meredith was placed on the transfer list, and was duly snapped up by Manchester United for a bargain £500 although his suspension had eighteen months to run. Three days after the signing, no less than seventeen City players were suspended for receiving illegal payments and barred from ever playing for City again (many of the group finished up with Meredith at the United.) That it was United players who formed one of the pockets of militancy in the players' strike of 1909, may not be entirely coincidental to Meredith's presence in the club either. Somehow, controversy did seem to follow him around.

Cup Final attendances had been around the 60,000 mark since the Spurs win of 1901, but they sprang back to over 100,000 when 1905 brought the best side in the country, Newcastle, to the Palace with a chance of completing the Double. To add further spice to the proceedings, their opponents were Aston Villa who had thrown away their own chances in the League by a poor start to the season but had run lately into form.

In the event it was Villa's day not Newcastle's. Howard Spencer, their veteran full back and captain was in commanding form, and in the centre forward role they had the dashing Harry Hampton, John Campbell's successor, and a young man who had changed the old Villa reliance on short passing by banging the ball out to the wings. The Newcastle defence never quite mastered Villa's long passes going from centre to wing and even from one wing over to the other, and Villa finished the day 2–0 winners.

Newcastle were later to see this result as the start of an un-canny sequence where they could win on almost any ground in the country except Crystal Palace. They played there the very next year against Everton who duly took the Cup 1–0. After a year's grace when Everton lost the Cup in turn in the Final of 1907 to Sheffield Wednesday, Newcastle were back to play Wolves.

This 1908 Final looked a foregone conclusion. From the largest entry yet of 348 clubs, only Wolves, a home-grown side who had finished well down the Second Division, stood between Tyne-side and the Cup. Newcastle were fielding a side with English, Scottish, and Irish internationals, and with six veterans from the 1906 Final determined that this was to be their year. On a wet dismal afternoon that kept the attendance down to 74,967, New-castle launched one sophisticated attack after another which Wolves somehow kept out. Then a Wolves centre from Harri-son on the right wing went loose, was collected by Hunt, the Wolves right half, and his long shot, more speculative than threatening, was helped into the net by the Newcastle goal-keeper. The Palace hoodoo had struck again. Two minutes later, the Wolves centre forward Hedley added another. 2–0. New-castle came back for the second half to grapple with the elements and the gremlins again and actually scored. But as they pressed forward for an equaliser, Harrison on the Wolves wing made more and more breakaway raids on their goal, culminating in a sixty yard dribble to score a third goal and to put the result beyond doubt at 3–1.

The following season, 1909, Manchester United and Billy Meredith came and took away the Cup by beating Bristol City 1–0. It was a rough and physical encounter from which only Meredith and Bristol City's centre half Wedlock emerged with their reputations unscathed.

1910 was, at last, Newcastle's year. But did they beat the Palace hoodoo? Alas no. They had to go through a tedious 1–1 draw notable for fouls and little else at the Palace, and the Cup was only theirs when they got their opponents Barnsley to a replay at Everton and then clinched the long-awaited Cup with some better football and a 2–0 victory.

One would have expected that to give them some sort of confidence when they returned to the Palace the following season to play Bradford City but no, again they played out a tedious and this time goal-less draw. And having been unable to win in the grand manner by laying the Palace ghost, they proved unable even to win the replay going down by the only goal, a goal in which their goalkeeper Lawrence aided and abetted.

The replay was held at Old Trafford on the following Wednesday, and an amusing sidelight on the pulling power of the Cup was recorded by Dr Percy Young in his history of Manchester United. On the Monday morning after the Bradford/Newcastle drawn game on the Saturday, a Manchester business house carried the following notice to employees:

> All requests for leave of absence on account of toothache, severe colds, and minor ailments, funerals, picnics, church socials, and the like, must be handed to the head of department before 10 a.m. on the morning of Wednesday's match.

The humour would have escaped Newcastle for in the seven years from 1905 to 1911, they played in five Finals and two Final Replays yet only won once, and that not at the Palace. In fairness to them, we must look at their prowess in the League for a more accurate picture of their abilities.

They won the League in 1905, 1907, and 1909 and their record for those years reads as follows:

1905 W–23 L–9 D–2 Goals For–72 Against–33 Points–48.
      (Everton second with 47 points)
1907 W–22 L–9 D–7 Goals For–74 Against–46 Points–51.
      (Bristol City second with 48 points)
1909 W–24 L–9 D–5 Goals For–65 Against–41 Points–53.
      (Everton second with 46 points)

Gaining much of their strength from two half-backs, Peter McWilliam and the versatile Colin Veitch who played at various times in six different forward and back positions, plus the quaintly nicknamed 'Dadler' Aitken at centre-half and 'Cockles' Appleyard at centre-forward, Newcastle had another more dubious claim to fame. Veitch and two club colleagues were the first to evolve an off-side strategy – it was possible before 1907 to be offside in one's own half and by pushing all the Newcastle players forward, it was possible to keep the opposition pinned in their own penalty area! When England applied the Newcastle idea against Scotland in the 1906 international, the Scots' plea to the International Board got the 1907 change to the sanctity of one's own half of the field.

Later Newcastle had to concede to their neighbours Sunderland. Sunderland's success rested largely on the latest and most famous of football triangles. They were only Champions twice, in 1902 and in 1913, but they finished third four times, and the names of three men come down to us with their high reputations unscathed – Cuggy, Mordue and Buchan. This 'infernal triangle' as it was known to opponents was composed of the three positions on the right half of the field, wing, half-back and inside-forward, with Charlie Buchan as the deadly inside-forward. It was a common enough formula but these three brought it to perfection. Buchan, a tall willowy youth, who joined the club in 1911 for £1,000, was exceptionally gifted with heading ability and in the 1913 Championship season scored 31 of the club's 86 goals himself.

Sunderland's presence at the Cup Final of 1913 with an opportunity of completing 'The Double' goes a long way to explaining the dramatic increase in attendance. Only 55,556 people had turned up to see the goal-less draw of 1912 between Barnsley and West Bromwich Albion, a dull and academic piece of non-football finally resolved at a Bramall Lane replay by

Barnsley's solitary goal. Barnsley's capacity to win only after a war of attrition had amply been demonstrated on their route to the Palace. In the Fourth Round, they 'drew' Bradford City in every sense of the word. The scores were 0–0, 0–0 after extra time, and then a goal glut which Barnsley won 3–2. But having found out how to score goals, they promptly forgot again and drew 0–0 with Swindon in the Semi-Final. It took another replay which they won 1–0, to get into the Final. Not exactly the stuff that either dreams or packed terraces are made of.

Now in 1913, the prospect of Sunderland playing Aston Villa, League Champions v the runners up, drew a record 120,081 people, a record that would be still with us but for the flimsy nature of the gates of Wembley Stadium forcibly opened and invaded in 1923. Against the infernal triangle, Villa had Sam Hardy in goal – poker-faced 'Silent Sam', and a line of half-backs in Barber, Harrop (who was said to pass like Harry Vardon putted) and Leach who could stop anything that moved. Bache on the left wing and Harry Hampton at centre forward were their main threats in attack.

The football, in the event, was more ruthless than artistic, affected as both teams were by the magnitude of the occasion. Hampton and Charlie Thompson, Sunderland's captain, came to blows and although they were not sent off, were both later suspended. Villa's Wallace nervously fluffed a penalty then turned before the end from villain to hero with a corner kick that met Barber's forehead to finish in the Sunderland net. Sunderland hit the post twice, Buchan, Martin and Richardson missed chances, some when Villa goalkeeper Hardy was temporarily off the field, but 1–0 to Villa it was and 1–0 it stayed. For the record, the crowd got their money's worth, for the game was timed as lasting 107 minutes. Sunderland went home and Villa took the Cup with them to the Palladium where they appeared with George Robey. No one in the audience needed to be told who they were but one doubts the veracity of the remark that is supposed to have been made in the gallery – 'I can see the Villa team but who is the man with the bowler hat and eyebrows?'

Attendances dropped again the following year to 72,778 but for the first time the reigning monarch, King George V, was among them and a precedent had been set for years to come. The final was decided between Burnley and Liverpool, Burnley scoring the solitary goal of the game, but one can be sure the public imagination generally was more enthusiastic about the fact that Royal approval of the national game had been so visibly demonstrated. Somehow it showed for all to see that as the era came near its grim close, the game that had started with the ordinary man, only to become a prerogative of the few, which had switched dramatically from a public school to a working class symbol, could now finally stage an annual fixture where the sovereign and his humblest subject could be seen alongside one another. Football no longer belonged to any class in particular, it was truly a national sport. Despite their frequent prevarication and their tardiness to recognise the economic facts of life, that this should be so it a tribute to the very real achievements of the Football Association. Of them it could perhaps be said that they got there in the end.

And when, on Monday November 27th 1972, the FA Council finally deleted the term 'amateur' from their rules, belated but welcome recognition of the true nature of the problems that had plagued their Edwardian forerunners, was complete.

By 1914 then, football could be said to be the national sport. It could not, however, be called the *inter*-national sport it is today. The series of internationals between the domestic countries were fully underway by 1890 – England v Scotland had the honour of being first in the field in 1870, Wales were next to join in by playing Scotland first in 1876 and England first in 1879, and in the eighties Ireland came into the fold playing England and Wales in 1882, and Scotland in 1884.

Once one has granted Wales credit for winning the International Championship in 1906–7 and Ireland for doing the same in 1913–4, the inherent weakness of their teams, unable to call on the depth of professional talent available to England and Scotland, is plain for all to see. Both countries made attempts to get the International Board to decree that League clubs should automatically release Irish and Welsh players when their country needed them, but in the teeth of powerful if myopic opposition from League clubs who paid the players and consequently demanded the employers' first call on their services, the most the Board could do was to make polite requests, suggestions and pleas. Meanwhile these two countries continued to lose. I need hardly add that the pattern is still with us.

Ireland from 1890 to 1914 played England 25 times, they drew 3 times, won twice in 1913 and 1914, and lost the other twenty, conceding 95 goals in the process and scoring a mere 20 themselves. And against Scotland they had an almost identical record, having played another 25 matches, drawing 2, winning 2 and losing the other 21, conceding 96 goals and scoring 20.

Wales in the same period did marginally better, which is like saying that it is better to be shot five times than ten times. Against England, their record reads P–25 W–0 D–5 L–20 Goals For–16 Goals Against–78, and against Scotland, P–25 W–4 D–7 L–14 Goals For–29 Goals Against–69. Small wonder then that Ireland and Wales generally played each other only for the honour of avoiding the wooden spoon. In that private battle, Wales won 11 matches and Ireland 10 with the remaining 4 drawn.

The major series of domestic competition was naturally between England and the Old Enemy. I do not propose to cover the matches for the story has been told wonderfully well in Brian James' book *England v Scotland* with a blend of explanatory comment and contemporary reportage that is in every way admirable, and in a detail which would be impossible here. Suffice it to say that eight of the matches were draws, England won 10 and Scotland won 7, England scored 41 goals and Scotland scored 32, but those bare statistics conceal some royal battles to stir the blood even seventy years on.

One of the most interesting features of the series is that although it could draw enormous crowds of a hundred thousand plus, it could only do so in Scotland – at the drawn game played at the Crystal Palace in March 1901 just two weeks before the Spurs v Sheffield United FA Cup Final, a crowd of less than 25,000 watched the international as against a crowd more than four times larger for the club game. Even by 1909, the crowd at the Palace for England's 2–0 victory was a bare 35,000 who saw it as a greater attraction than that day's Boat Race. This was not a feature of metropolitan indifference alone, for in those days the England home matches were shared around the country in a more equitable fashion than today with Blackburn, Liverpool, Birmingham, Sheffield, and Newcastle all getting a chance to play host to the game in turn.

Probably there were two factors involved – the parochialism of

the average English football supporter who did not wish to look
beyond his own particular club and for whom the concept of
an England team did not have the magic of their local heroes,
and also the capacity of one particular sport to become identified
with a small nation's destiny when precious little else on the
social scene presents itself.

With this latter factor in mind, is it not possible to see something in common between Scottish attitudes to soccer, and Welsh
attitudes to rugby? In both cases, the game, be it soccer or
rugby, was played supremely well and became the national focus
for alleviating slights, some imagined but many real, and a substitute that went some way to compensate for inabilities to compete on level terms at the more important social and economic
levels.

A Welsh defeat at soccer or a Scottish defeat at rugby can be
treated by the local populations with relative shoulder-shrugging
indifference, but for the Welsh to lose at rugby or the Scots at
soccer is akin to a national disaster. And to lose to England is the
unkindest cut of all. Jokes about Scotsmen feeling ten feet tall
in dark blue jerseys, and Welsh hearts beating faster encased
in scarlet shirts, have a very real point so long as so much
store is placed upon what is, after all, a game. History, as a
wiser man than I once remarked, is rarely about what actually
happened but far more about what people *think* actually happened. And until the Scots and the Welsh *think* they are on a
completely level social and economic footing with the English,
the store placed on Scotland beating England at soccer and Wales
beating England at rugby, is unlikely to wither. For good and
sometimes for ill, it is the unspoken but deeply felt senses of
grievance off the field, that has brought the passion and the
colour to those particular sporting series.

Beyond these shores, others were beginning to find football
attractive. In Denmark, Austria, Italy, France, Germany, Holland
and others, the game played originally by British expatriates
began to attract the local populations, and they, unlike the
British, did not seek to go it alone but rather sought to organise
on an international basis. Because, as in industry, the British
had been first in the field, it was to the Football Association
that these bodies looked for a lead.

In 1902, the Dutch FA approached the FA to discuss the

foundation of an International Association to promote football in Europe. They wrote to the FA in the spring, got a lukewarm reply that the matter would be discussed by the International Board, and it was only in April 1903 that the Dutch were informed that the proposal would be passed on to the Scottish, Welsh and Irish Associations for their consideration.

The French meanwhile were coming independently to a similar conclusion and a letter was received in November 1903 from the Union des Sports Athletiques proposing the setting up of a Federation of European Football Associations. The FA '. . . cannot see the advantages of such a Federation . . .' the French were told. In this most insular of times, when all things foreign were rejected out of hand because they *were* foreign and British was best, so narrow sighted a rejoinder is not surprising. It was an attitude which elevated the horse over the motor car and the art of the Royal Academy over that of the Cubists, though its full repercussions in the smaller world of football were not to be felt until later years.

In the early part of 1904, the FA Secretary Wall was instructed to sound out the County Associations on the possibility of an international conference in England, but by then, the Europeans had decided to go ahead on their own. On May 21, 1904 a Congress of Paris comprising representatives from France, Belgium, Switzerland, Netherlands, Denmark, Sweden and Spain, set up the Federation Internationale de Football Association, to be better known as FIFA.

In a matter of days, an FA committee had been set up to examine foreign developments and again to examine the possibility of a conference in England, not one feels because these continentals were to be encouraged but because it might prove embarrassing if British clubs started to undertake continental tours (Tottenham had been refused FA permission to tour Germany in 1901). And to let the foreigners know that their pioneering was not necessarily appreciated, the FA refused an invitation to send a team to compete for the international cup donated by Count Carl van der Straten Pouthoy.

Robert Guerin of France made two visits to London to persuade the FA to take a lead in the development of the new association but on both occasions, he found the English attitude, as he said later, 'incomprehensible'.

With that maddening mixture of ignorance and arrogance that was to signify so many of England's dealings abroad, in 1905 the FA decided to stay outside of the new body, but gave their consent, on conditions and twelve months late, to its being formed! It was not until awareness dawned that FIFA might have un-English ways of running affairs – would they define amateurs as we do? and similar problems – that the FA took a more positive attitude and deigned to send representatives along to a FIFA conference in June 1906.

The continentals who could, one feels, have been forgiven for sending them back to England with nasty foreign fleas in their ears, behaved in a considerably more statesmanlike fashion. Not only did they agree to draft a new constitution to conform to FA conventions, they elected FA representative Woolfall as their President for 1906–7. In 1908 too, they preserved the FA from embarrassment by refusing to recognise the breakaway Amateur Football Association, and although they were originally reluctant to allow Scotland, Ireland and Wales into their councils (for it appeared an underhanded way of increasing English voting power), they retracted and welcomed them in in 1910.

Only three years later did the British reciprocate and admit two FIFA men to the International Board with full voting rights. And the entente remained cordiale only until the twenties when the British Associations withdrew from FIFA over a squabble on varying definitions of the amateur until after the Second World War, which is why the World Cup was something played for exclusively by foreigners until relatively recently. (And if anyone finds a parallel in the whole sad tale and Britain's long drawn out will she, won't she, negotiations over the Common Market, he is welcome to do so.)

Consequently, as world football grew, and Italians, Hungarians and Brazilians brought new methods and flair to the game that started in Britain, British horizons were defined by the top of the bob-bank and her football orthodoxies became quietly passé. When the Hungarians wreaked a six-goal havoc at Wembley, and ninety years of so-called home supremacy vanished in a traumatic ninety minutes on a November afternoon in 1953, all possibility of the result being a fluke dispelled six months later in Budapest in the face of another seven Hungarian goals in the

English net, the shock was all the more profound for being totally unexpected. Yet how predictable it all was, based as it was on the deep suspicion of all things foreign that lay at the heart of Edwardian insularity, and on the perpetuation of that most damaging of all Edwardian myths that British was bound to be best.

CHAPTER THREE

The RFU Do It Their Way

As the 1880s drew to a close, rugby football presented a far from united front. England and Scotland particularly were at odds with one another, there had been no International Championship since the 1886–87 season, and the strains between the working class approaches of men in the north of England, and the more aristocratic and public school coloured views of the South, which we have already seen in association football, were inevitably reflected in rugby, perhaps more so. They were to come to a head as dramatically as they had in soccer, and arguably with more lasting results.

In rugby as in association football, England and Scotland had been the first countries to play internationals against one another starting with the 1870–71 season, but although this particular annual battle is dignified by one of sport's more graceful trophies, the Calcutta Cup, that was not donated until 1878.

Interestingly enough, the trophy, of Indian chased workmanship, came not from success but from failure. Some old Rugbeians (whose attempt to start rugby football in, of all places, Calcutta, had foundered on the popularity of polo and lawn tennis), had used the surplus funds accumulated by their short-lived club to donate a cup to the Rugby Union specifically to keep the name of Calcutta in rugby annals.

Ireland were next to join in in 1874–5 yet Wales, amazingly with her later affinity for the game in mind, played first at international level only in the 1880–81 season. (France was even later on the scene when England visited Paris first in 1905–06.)

No doubt rejoicing jointly that they were the pioneers, England and Scotland failed to set much of an example of international cordiality. The distinguished series came to a temporary halt after England's second successive victory, by one goal to one try, at

Blackheath in the 1883–84 season. England had slightly the worse of the match although containing the lively Scottish forwards better than had been expected. As was the contemporary custom, both teams played nine forwards each, and these eighteen forwards saw most of the ball and most of the play. Reid of Edinburgh Academicals scored Scotland's try, that no one questioned. The dispute was over England's try which was duly goaled to win the match. One of the Scottish players, at a line-out, was guilty of a 'knock-back' which was seized by the Englishmen for Kindersley, an Oxford and Devon forward, to bustle over the line. The referee allowed a try. Scotland vehemently protested the legality of the award.

The dispute only makes some sort of sense if we interpret the 'knock-back' as what we would call a 'knock-on', a common enough occurence at a line-out in all conscience. The law as it then stood did not mention 'knocking-back' but it did talk of 'knocking-on'. Passed in 1874 the law said this:

> "Knocking on", i.e. *deliberately* hitting the ball with the hand, and "throwing forward" i.e. throwing the ball in the direction of the opponent's goal-line are not lawful. If the ball be either "knocked on" or "thrown forward", the captain of the opposing side *may* . . . require to have it brought back to the spot where it was so knocked or thrown on and there put down. (My italics)

In 1883, that is the year before the disputed try, the law had been amended and 'deliberately' had been deleted. As England saw it, the points at issue were these.

1. That it was lawful to 'knock-back'.
2. That even if it was illegal to do so the Scotsmen could claim no advantage from an illegal act committed by one of their own side.
3. That as no Englishman appealed, the subsequent play was legal.
4. That the referee decided that a try was obtained, and based his decision on a point of fact put before him being whether an Englishman had appealed or not.

I take this quotation from that invaluable early book on the game, *Rugby Union Football* edited by the Reverend F. Marshall, 1892 edition, page 178. Marshall also tells us that

> The Scotsmen contended that "the point in dispute was the interpretation of the law dealing with knocking the ball, and denied the right of the Rugby Union to be sole interpreters of the laws of the game". The Rugby Union, for the sake of argument conceded the Scotch interpretation of the law, viz. "that knocking back was illegal", but firmly refused the decision of the referee on a point of fact to be submitted to any arbitration.

If I am correct in thinking that the 'knock-back' was indeed a knock-on, it is possible to see some right on both sides in this apparently trivial dispute. The Scots were correct in thinking that an offence had been committed, for the deletion of the word 'deliberately' made any knock-on illegal. Also there was no such thing as an advantage rule – that, and the abolition of the necessity of claiming for an offence – did not come until 1896. On the other hand, the amended law as it read in 1883 said that the opposing captain *may* require etc, it did not say he *had* to – a kind of advantage rule in its own right. Again, the English view that the referee should not be subject to arbitration on points of fact which he alone could properly judge, was obviously wise. On the other hand, the Scots had a very good point that the right of interpretation of knotty points should not be an English monopoly.

As the debate continued between the warring factions, acrimony over the issue led to the abandonment of the England v Scotland fixture for the 1884–5 season. It was resumed for two years with a scoreless draw in 1886 and another draw, both sides scoring a try, in 1887, but the full shock waves of Kindersley's now notorious try or non-try were to continue to reverberate for the rest of the decade.

Ireland offered to play the role of peacemaker between the quarrelling sides with the result that representatives from England and Scotland met on neutral ground in Dublin to settle the dispute. Scotland suggested that they would at last formally concede England's 1884 Richmond victory by virtue of Kindersley's try, but only providing that the English Rugby Union would join with them, Ireland and Wales, in forming an International

Board which would settle disputes on points of law, and which would be the ultimate authority overseeing international fixtures.

Suspicions that the English were in some way likely to be taken for a ride by low Celtic and Gaelic cunning, if such a body were democratically constituted, the English representatives were adamant that they would not join such a body unless they did so on terms more favourable than the other home countries. The Rugby Union also aggravated the situation by unilaterally writing the penalty kick into the laws in 1888. (The early laws had talked of and catalogued infringements of various kinds, but without providing a punishment for the crime. Probably offenders were given an unofficial hack across the shins to make them mend their manners*, otherwise a scrummage to restart the game sufficed.)

A sort of penalty had been introduced for offside in 1882 but it was then called a 'free kick', and that meant a drop kick or a punt, but not at the posts for no goal could be scored from it. This idea was gradually applied to other offences, as a matter of convenience, and no one found any reason to object. The novel feature of the new law passed by the Rugby Union in 1888 was that such a free kick could now be 'awarded by way of penalty', could be taken as a place kick, and a goal could be scored from it.**

Scotland and Ireland were strongly prejudiced against the new penalty particularly as it applied to a knock-on at a line-out. With this fuel added to the flames of the row over representation on the International Board to be set up, events reached a total impasse. Scotland, Ireland and Wales set up a Board and continued to play one another while England were left without an international. That the concept of a penalty could lead to so much unpleasantness is difficult to understand unless we remember the similar rumpus in association football three years later when the public school men saw such an award as an affront to their sense of honour and fair play. Both the Scottish and the Irish rugby teams at this stage were composed entirely of University and public school or boarding school and day academy

*Whether the hack in such cases came from an opponent or a team-mate one does not know.

**See Admiral Sir Percy Royds' *The History of the Laws of Rugby Football*, 1949, p. 175.

men*, and it was they who were adamant that such an offence would not be committed deliberately because such conduct would be unbecoming a gentleman and a sportsman – such stigma alone would be sufficient a deterrent.

It was partly to soccer that rugby looked for a solution for two men, Lord Kingborough and Major Marindin (President of the FA until 1889), were appointed as mutually acceptable arbitrators in the dispute. They reported in April 1890 and their recommendations were used as the basis for a newly constituted International Board to replace the old one. Henceforward the Board was to administer all internationals which were to be played under one code, any disputes arising from matches could be settled by a simple Board majority, but amendments to the laws themselves could only be effected by virtue of three-quarters of the representatives present being in favour of a change. The tricky problem of equality of representation was settled by England being allowed to make up half the Board of twelve, this on the basis that they had far more clubs under their jurisdiction than anyone else, while the other three countries supplied two representatives each to complete the other half. As a sop to Scotland and Ireland, the arbitrators also wrote in a clause that the Rugby Union laws would be adopted generally, except that the objectionable penalty would not be awarded scoring points.

Points as a method of deciding rugby matches were another bone of contention. In the original laws played at Rugby School where the game, albeit in a rudimentary form, was born, matches were decided by the first side to obtain two goals. If this happy seal to the players' labours was not possible after five *day's* play (!) or no goals had been kicked by either side after three *day's* play, the match was drawn. This is how matters stood, officially at least, until a Rugby Union ruling of 1874 that a match could be decided by a majority of goals. That rule lasted a bare twelve months until another edict was issued that if the number of goals were equal, the deciding factor was to be a majority of tries.

Whether that led to confusion or not is unclear, but for some reason it was thought necessary in 1877 to add a rider that in

---

*In the 1899 edition of the Badminton Library, *Football*, it was said succinctly that in Scotland 'Rugby is the game of the classes; the masses are devoted to Association'.

the event of a goal being kicked from a try, only the goal counted. (Three years before a radical suggestion that scoring should be counted in points proved too revolutionary a concept and was duly rejected.)

It took until 1886 for the authorities to announce that henceforward the score would be in points – three points for a goal (of any kind, whether a try had been scored first or not) and one point for a try. An attempt to make a goaled try worth more than any other goal drew the memorable remark from the Rugby Union that this was something they 'would always oppose and . . . trust will never be sanctioned'. The sanction came just three years later in 1889 as the Rugby Union stood on its head to announce a new set of point values – three points for a goal, two points for a penalty goal, one point for an ungoaled try.

The original International Board, without England as a member, had another set – four points for a goal from a try, three points for a dropped goal or a goal from a mark, and two points for a try, but they, as we have seen, did not allow penalties.

The newly constituted Board, with England in, went in 1891 for two point tries, three point penalty goals, five points for a goaled try, and four points for any other kind of goal. This was then adopted by the other Unions, but the fun did not stop there, for in 1893 England and Wales adopted three point tries, and in 1894 the International Board adopted it from them. And after Scotland's failure in 1900 to get the penalty reduced to two points, 1905 saw the adoption of the values that were to last until 1948, for the 'any other goal' was made three points while the dropped goal remained at four points.

With this confused and confusing catalogue of dates and points stretching over years, it is not surprising that at the Cardiff Arms Park on January 7th, 1893, when Wales beat England by one goal, one penalty goal and two tries to one goal and three tries, half of the Welsh crowd chaired their heroes all the way to the adjoining Angel Hotel, rejoicing in a victory by 12 points to 11, while the other half were left wondering why so much fuss was being made over a 14 points all draw! A Welsh victory it was by the first of the two scores, but there must have been many a similar dilemma at club level before scoring values became universal.

Such confusion is ample evidence that the game as we know

it was having an anxious and confusing birth. Admiral Royds records a delightful example of confusion, appeal and counter appeal at an 1887 match between Leeds Parish Church and Wakefield Trinity (at this stage very much a union club). A ball thrown in from touch rebounded into the air from a Wakefield forward's chest. Before it reached the ground, a Leeds back fly-hacked at it and sent it freakishly over the Wakefield crossbar. Amid Leeds jubilation, the barrack-room lawyers of the Trinity side got going. Not over the crossbar, they said. Yes it was, said the referee. In that case, it was a punt, they said. No, said the referee, a punt is when one drops the ball from the hands and kicks it before it touches the ground. In that case, said Wakefield, the throw-in from touch was not straight. Quite right, said the referee, but you should have appealed for that in the first place – the score stands and it is your kick-off!

Much of such confusion must have stemmed from the casual nature of early rugby for if the essence of soccer is simplicity, the key to rugby is its relative sophistication. If an intelligent Martian were placed on the touchline and asked to watch either game, it is reasonable to surmise that without aid he would be able at the end of ninety minutes to have at least an approximate grasp of soccer with the possible exception of the offside rule. On the other hand, one suspects eighty minutes of rugby would leave him as baffled and unaware of some of the major features of the game as he was in the first five minutes. This is not to say either code is superior or inferior to the other, merely that they are very different despite their common ancestry.

Although rugby throughout its history has tended to be deeply conservative and resistant to change, changes have in fact been frequent, an inevitable concomitant of evolution and growing sophistication. To recapture the spirit of high Victorian rugby and early international matches, one has to make a conscious effort to imagine a field packed with players – twenty a side was universal until the Oxford v Cambridge match of 1875 used XVs, a method followed at international level in the 1876–77 season and ever since.

The result of this Malthusian over-population, and exponents who were in no way specialists, must have been a spectacle akin to a band of schoolboys or army recruits given a rugby ball for the first time and told to get on with it. Unable in their ignorance to anticipate where the ball will be in ten seconds time, everyone clusters to the spot where the ball is at that moment, and one heaving, amorphous mass of humanity, like wasps swarming around a jam-pot, wends a slow and predictable path up and down the field, the ball rarely in view at all.

With this formless picture in mind, I suspect it is possible to understand the alarm of some pioneers when hacking of opponents' shins became illegal. As late as 1889, the law relating to scrummaging defined the object of a scrum thus – '. . . by kicking the ball, to drive it in the direction of the opposite goal line'. And the offside law, passed originally in 1874, but holding sway for long afterwards, said a man was offside if '. . . being in a scrummage (he) gets in front of the ball . . .' Reading between the lines, it is obvious that the front lines of such scrummages were firing lines composed of half a dozen and more men on either side kicking furiously at the ball and each others' shins trying desperately to drive the ball onwards and the men defending backwards. It was the perfect theatre for the display of all the Muscular Christians' manly virtues – a stage on which to receive and return in abundance knocks, hacks and kicks without flinching. In these circumstances, hacking was morally desirable and of practical necessity.

It cannot be emphasised enough that the concept of hooking the ball and heeling it back was not only unheard of, but would have been illegal if anyone had attempted it, for that would have put players on one's own team 'off their side'. Even to put a head down to look for the ball before directing a kick in its general direction was *infra dig*. Arthur Budd, a forward first capped for England against Ireland in 1878, has left eloquent testimony to the philosophy:

A player who could not take and give hacks was not considered worth his salt, and to put one's head down in a scrummage was regarded as an act of high treason.*

Such attitudes died hard, but from the roots of so barbarian and incoherent an activity the 1890s saw the growth of a new and more fluent form of rugby football resembling our own. There were intermediate stages. From the tight hacking melees of the 1860s, forwards, particularly after the banishing of ten

*Marshall 1892 edition, p. 115.

of the forty players on the field, began to kick the ball around between themselves and into the newly won spaces. Then they gradually learned to make short passes between themselves to progress down the field. From that it was a natural development for the ball to be passed betweeen the halfbacks, then for the halves occasionally to part with the ball to the three-quarters, and eventually for the three-quarters to pass it among themselves (although there are those who would say the last-named stage has yet to be universally recognised!)

The role of the backs through these developments changed from something akin to patient spectators waiting for the ball to pop out of the melée like a pip from a lemon, to quietly replacing the forwards as front-line troops expected to administer the final *coup de grace*.

Attempts have been made to credit individuals with specific inventions in tactics – J. Payne in a North v South match of 1881 was said by some to have been the first half-back ever to pass to a three-quarter (!) and Alan Rotherham of Oxford and Richmond is generally acknowledged to have been the first half-back to interpret his function as being a link between the three-quarters and the source of supply. Without wishing to take anything away from men who must have been just that little more forward-looking than their fellows, it is probably more accurate to see the developments as inevitable ones. At first, any back who got the ball would chance his arm, or rather his leg, at a drop for goal. Gradually it dawned that a passing movement leading to a try was more profitable, but one doubts that ideas like this did have an actual inventor. More likely is that in different areas, players found different solutions *extempore* as new situations arose in the course of play.

Gradually as the new practices filtered into the body politic, they became incorporated into the game generally, either formally in the way of a new law or casually by force of custom if they were generally thought to be healthy, or alternatively discarded or banned if they were found ineffective or smacked of sharp practice.

Punch in July 1908 poked fun at the Rules of Golf, and referred to the 'two octavo volumes containing Rule 27 relating to casual water'. Certainly to the uninitiated, golf rules present a formidable undergrowth of paragraphs, sub-paragraphs, notes, addenda, sections and sub-sections, but the reason is that as the years passed, the original simple code no longer sufficed for as more and more people played, more and more new occurrences needed interpretation. In exactly the same way, the laws of rugby have spread themselves vastly as years have gone by, so that they now embody a deal of case-law that at first glance is quite beyond the grasp of the average player.

It could be said that this is a weakness, and certainly legal prose does not make for light reading, but I think it is also a strength, and that we are near to understanding a crucial difference between the development of rugby and the development of soccer.

In soccer, part of its rich variety comes from the way different regions and countries have played the game. Hungarians, Brazilians, Liverpudlians and Cockneys have brought something of their own to soccer in the way they play the same game. In rugby, this has also happened obviously and the different patterns of play between, say, the Welsh, the English and the New Zealanders, are striking. But I think it is also true that different regions and countries have come to rugby over the years and made it overall into a living amalgam of their often quite contrary attitudes. It is not only a game they have *played,* it is also a game they have *made.* Thanks to the Welsh, we have four three-quarters; thanks to the English we have forwards prepared to wheel the ball from a scrummage; thanks ironically to the New Zealanders' temporary departure from the norm, we have scrummages of eight forwards. These are just a few examples where many more could be cited.

The corollary to the compromises the game has made to its differing exponents is the conflict which has attended them, for, for every faction which has wished to pull the game in a particular direction, there have been those who prophesied ruin and who firmly resisted the pull. The development of back play was gloomily thought by many to be the end of all good forward play, and the opening of the door to milksops and weaklings. Budd thought that passing was 'an epidemic' and 'a contagion', and that 'exaggerated efforts to imitate the inventors ... (have) reduced the system to a burlesque'. Reactions to the penalty we have already discussed.

It was ever thus. For every radical who sprang up, there were always five conservatives who wanted to quash him, and the subject was generally decided on the question of whose persistence faltered first. However, conflicts on points of rugby law and tactics pale into insignificance compared with the crisis which reached its height in 1893. It was, of course, rugby coming to face the problem that had seen so much blood metaphorically spilled at the soccer code, the amateur/professionalism question.

If the public school ethic was strong in soccer, its strength was that of ten in rugby. It is easy to see why. If the Muscular Christians and their disciples in the public schools, given sufficient wit, had been asked to invent a game that exhausted boys before they could fall victims to vice and idleness, which at the same time instilled the manly virtues of absorbing and inflicting pain in about equal proportions, which elevated the team above the individual, which bred courage, loyalty and discipline, which as yet had no taint of professionalism, and which, as an added bonus, occupied thirty boys at a time instead of a mere twenty-two, it is probably something like rugby that they would have devised.

As it happened they did not need to invent it, merely to adopt it. And because the populace in the industrial north did not take the game up to the extent that they did soccer, the Barbarian and Philistine classes kept it. (Soccer had going for it its basic simplicity and immediate appeal and also that it did not need special clothing or specially designed goalposts for a quickly organised casual game. Curiously, rugby was actually nearer to the people's football from which the two codes had emerged.) For those middle and upper-middle classes, rugby became a symbol of their moral attitudes and a banner waving bravely in the breeze of the amateur spirit.

Although it is generally accurate that the masses did not take to rugby as they did to association, that was not true everywhere. No doubt in the Welsh valleys, in Yorkshire, in Liverpool, and in the West Country the first people ever to play rugby were public school old boys wishing to continue in later days what had become a way of life at school, or perhaps schoolboys on vacation. Either way, the local populations saw the game, liked what they saw, and took it up themselves. And uninhibited as they were by the conservatism and the wish to conform of the average schoolboy, they tended to play it inordinately well in a very short time.

89

Frequent allegations were made throughout the eighties that underground professionalism was on the increase, particularly in Yorkshire and Lancashire. It was not real professionalism, one can be sure, but rather clubs compensating their players for the inevitable loss of wages that resulted from Saturday afternoons spent on the rugby field rather than at the factory bench. The debate on such an issue was not however conducted in terms of practicalities but, as in soccer, in terms of morality. To a man like Budd, the issue was quite clear. He wrote in 1892;

> The answer . . . to those who urge that the working man ought to be compensated for the "loss of time" incurred by his recreation is that, if he cannot afford the leisure to play a game, he must do without it.

In the face of what he saw as an encroaching evil, he urged administrators to hold fast, for;

> To them the charge of a game of great traditions has been committed, and, if they would be willing to consign the future of those to the baneful influence of professionalism, they would assuredly be betraying the trust reposed in them and live regretfully to see the game of today depraved, degraded and decayed.

There were many to echo his words before the events of 1893 and afterwards. In both the 1899 and 1904 editions of Montague Shearman's *Football History,* an anonymous chapter on rugby claims that professionalism means submersion of the amateur, the creation of 'a comparatively idle class on the community', ruin to those who adopt it as a profession, and the 'elimination of all sport from the game'.

I shall give the events of the early 1890s as they occurred, and as evidence of the virulence the morality of the issue could arouse, I shall include some comments made by George Berney thirty years later in the 1925 edition of Marshall's book revised by L. R. Tosswill.

The loss of time payments made in Yorkshire ('veiled professionalism . . . was creeping on like a cancer in the body politic' – Berney.) was discussed at a number of Rugby Union meetings. In 1891, the issue was debated and suspicions were also expressed that something of a transfer system could be detected in the moves of good players from club to club. Out of the meeting and the discussion came regulations regarding transfer of membership from club to club, and a bye-law that only totally amateur clubs could be considered eligible for membership of the Rugby Union. But the matter did not end there.

Gate receipts continued to increase in Lancashire and Yorkshire, so although the new regulations may have received lip-service, unofficial 'broken-time' payments continued to be paid by many clubs. And clubs in those areas were themselves on the increase as the popularity of the game spread. The more working men participants there were, the more under-cover payments were made. ('... the players of the North at that time were chiefly of the type which – in these counties at all events – is accustomed to value its activities of whatever kind, in terms of cash when there is any about' – Berney.)

Neither these players nor their officials felt that the Rugby Union, largely composed of public school men, either understood their very real economic problems, or were prepared to let them play a full part in running rugby football. At a September 1891 meeting, a proposal that meetings should be held alternately in the North and South to enable those deterred by the cost and inconvenience of a journey to London to play a fuller part in affairs, got a majority but not the two-thirds necessary to put it into effect. The Reverend Francis Marshall, who was a stern upholder of the amateur principle, proposed and got carried regulations regarding transfers and a Rugby Union veto of leagues – because of the three year old Football League seen as a bastard child of professionalism, the very idea of leagues was anathema at rugby headquarters.

There matters rested for a while until a March 1893 meeting of a Rugby Union Committee which banned David and Evan James, the diminutive Swansea and Wales half-back pair who had found their way to Manchester under suspicious circumstances. (They were later reinstated as amateurs but after playing in a few more Welsh internationals, they returned to Manchester, took well paid jobs and played rugby for Broughton Rangers – the jobs and the rugby appearing about as coincidental as the £250 signing-on fee.)

At the September 20th, 1893 general meeting at the Westminster Palace Hotel it was fully anticipated that there would be a further collision between the Southern forces, for whom amateurism was sacred, and the particularly Yorkshire forces better aware of the true state of affairs in their area. ('The Yorkshire Committee . . . included members who were tainted with professionalism'—Berney.)

Many Northern delegates travelled down specifically to vote for just one proposal. Drafted in beguiling simple terms, its passing would have been a milestone in the game's history. Proposed by J. A. Millar and seconded by M. Newsome, both of Yorkshire, the proposal was;

> That players be allowed compensation for *bona fide* loss of time.

Before the proposal could be discussed, an amendment was put before the meeting by the Rugby Union secretary G. Rowland Hill* and seconded by R. S. Whalley of Lancashire;

> That this meeting, believing that the above principle is contrary to the true interest of the game and its spirit, declines to sanction the same.

The atmosphere must have been extremely tense as various and predictable arguments were placed before the meeting. Hill, Marshall and their friends dwelt on the evils of professionalism ('twin lode-stars, steel-blue eyes of truth and courage that radiated with the fire of nervous energy and the light of battle . . . the man who, with bell, book and candle faced the evil spirit of professionalism in Yorkshire . . . set out to checkmate the forces of evil' was Berney's description of Marshall) while the Yorkshiremen tried to make their Southern colleagues grasp the genuine predicament of many of their players.

If the North had done its best to get its representatives to London for the crucial vote, the South had not been idle either. A private committee had been formed before the meeting to drum up votes for the amateur cause, and the vote was finally swayed when H. E. Steed of Lennox produced 120 proxy votes from absentee clubs in support of the amendment. The amendment was carried by 282 votes to 136 votes. (Why the 136 votes should be found by Berney, a 'faggot vote', a slur repeated by the

---

*'Amateur of amateurs and Tory of Tories' as he was described in his *Times* obituary.

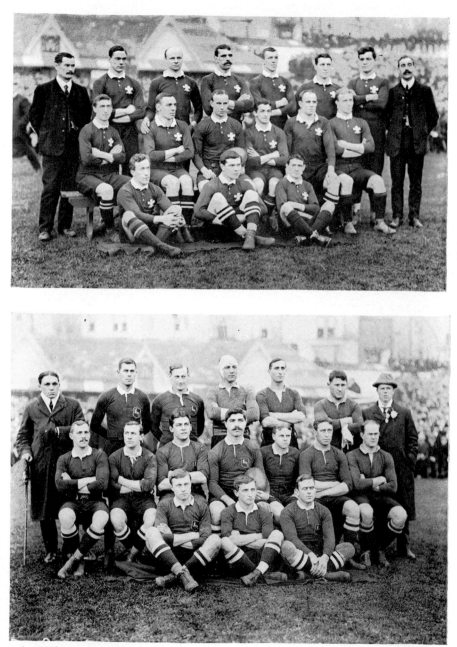

The Wales and the South Africa teams, loins girded and ready for their 1906 battle.
Note that the South Africans are bigger men and that for favourites, Wales look
somewhat apprehensive as if they knew sixty odd years would pass without a
victory over the Springboks

The South African forwards win possession from the line-out against Wales at Swansea in December 1906 on their way to an 11–0 victory

A gathering of Past and Present Harlequins in April 1922. J. G. Birkett (third from right front row) and Adrian Stoop (fifth from right front row) having helped to stage a revival of fortunes for Harlequins and England could rest content in the knowledge that in Wavell Wakefield (second row directly behind Stoop) they had a worthy successor as a tactician

English club rugby 1912 style. Against Blackheath the Rosslyn Park forwards, their backs idle spectators somewhere on the right, start a forward dribble down the touchline

A famous painting of Lord's in the late 1880s. Garrett of Australia fields a cover drive from W. G. Grace. Aiding and abetting on the long-off boundary are the Prince and Princess of Wales (on the right, with top-hat and parasol), Lord Harris (striped blazer, extreme left) is more interested in Lady de Grey than in the cricket, and the Prince is probably wondering if he can find a discreet way of joining Mrs Langtry (looking directly at the painter in the second row of seats)

Balliol Salmon's drawing of the fashions on parade at the Eton *v* Harrow match at Lord's in 1908

England's team, not a clean-shaven man amongst them, to play the First Test against Australia in 1896. From left to right – Top row: Lilley, Hearne, Gunn, Hayward. Second row: Richardson, Jackson, Grace, Lohmann, Stoddart. Front row: Brown and Abel. The absence of Ranjitsinhji provoked a controversy despite an England victory by six wickets. Five men in the picture refused to play in the Final Test unless their fee was raised

The autocrat of many a touring team's breakfast table – Yorkshire's Lord Hawke as he looked in a 1903 portrait

Below left: The tiny Indian and his friend the athletic Englishman. Ranjitsinhji and C. B. Fry, a Sussex batting partnership to break the heart of the most industrious and optimistic bowler

Below right: Australia's graceful batsman, the handsome Victor Trumper

Three views of W. G. Grace, the most eminent of Victorians. The 1913 photograph has an avuncular quality lacking in the full length painting by Stuart Wortley of 1890, although the brown shoes add a homely touch. The caption scribbled in the corner of the caricature, which is how Max Beerbohm saw the Doctor, reads 'Portrait of Dear Old WG – to the left is the Grand Stand; to the right, the funeral of one of his patients'

Left: The bowler who became an opening batsman, Yorkshire's Wilfred Rhodes, one of the greatest of all round cricketers. *Right:* B. J. T. Bosanquet of Middlesex and England whose invention of the googly was strangely neglected in England but found many adherents in South Africa

Not a male voice choir at an Edwardian smoking concert but the 1907–8 English team touring Australia. Top row, left to right: Young, Hayes, Fielder, Blythe, Humphries, Hobbs. Second row: Crawford, Braund, A. O. Jones (captain), Fane, Hutchings, Rhodes. Front row: Barnes, Hardstaff, Colonel Philip Trevor (manager), G. Gunn

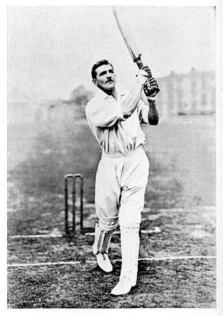

Left: The deadly left arm of
Colin Blythe of Kent and
England, a player plagued
by illness and a frail
physique, he lost his life in
the First World War.
Right: C. B. Fry, the
classicist and athlete who
made himself into a great
batsman

Jack Hobbs circa 1914, the
professional batsman who,
it was said, batted like an
amateur

English Rugby Union's latest official historians, U. Titley and R. McWhirter*, and the 282 votes perfectly democratic, escapes me.)

Despite the comfortable nature of the majority, immediately the General Meeting was closed a Special General Meeting was held and new lines of procedure adopted for General Meetings, ('. . . to crush any attempt to establish professional cells within the government machine'—Berney). After that, no one in Yorkshire could believe that they had any chance of persuading the Rugby Union to their cause, but for the next two years the major Yorkshire and Lancashire clubs stayed in the Rugby Union. (The two years is worth emphasising for many accounts make it sound as if the 21 clubs who eventually formed the Northern Union broke away from the parent body two minutes after the meeting closed.) Northern forwards continued to supply the bulk of England's international pack, a fact for which not everyone was grateful – 'Between the type of player developed under such influences and men of purely amateur ideals, the unity which is vital to the existence of team spirit could not survive, and consequently the cohesion of the National Fifteen degenerated' was Mr Berney's view.

Flushed with the success of the famous amendment of 1893, the Rugby Union got tougher and tougher and determined to purge itself of those who talked money in any form at the shrine of amateurism. A special committee drafted a new set of even tougher laws on amateur requirements and on the inadvisability of clubs competing on a league basis. These were to be placed before the General Meeting of September 19th 1895. Before that meeting could take place to give inevitable confirmation to the proposals, twenty-one clubs (9 from Lancashire and 12 from Yorkshire) met at the George Hotel, Huddersfield on August 29th, 1895 ('. . . at the Mitre Hotel, Leeds'—Berney) and formed a breakaway Northern Rugby Football Union on the broken-time principle. Three years later, payments for players, providing they were in other employment, was conceded.

The course of events, therefore, had proved conclusively that payment for broken time was only the first step towards professionalism as it has existed since then, and that the

The Centenary History of the Rugby Football Union by U. A. Titley and Ross McWhirter 1970.

verdict delivered by the Rugby Union in 1893 was absolutely right.*

This conclusion by U. A. Titley and Ross McWhirter is a comforting one for those who still adhere to the philosophy that there is something morally superior about amateurism, but surely it could equally be argued that if that broken-time resolution had been passed, not rejected, rugby might have grown to rival soccer as a national sport?** This is inevitably hypothetical, and no one can prove the point one way or the other. Perhaps it would be futile to explore the thesis further, but all the historical evidence is that the split, which might otherwise have been avoided, had at least two harmful effects.

Firstly, it robbed English rugby of a host of able players who put their talents at the services of the quite different game of rugby league which grew out of the break-away. (It is no coincidence that England were unable thereafter to produce a strong team until the last few seasons before the First World War.) Secondly, it meant that English rugby for far too long became identified, and some would say still is, with a narrow section of society. Because of this, the public school philosophy that to allow competitive games, knock-out competitions or coaching was tantamount to admitting professionalism held sway right up to our own day. What might have been a growth to fulfil the needs of many, was artificially stifled and kept back to preserve the game for a fortunate few. Unlike the case in soccer, the attempt to keep the masses out of the Edwardian rugby garden succeeded all too well. By that we have all been the losers.

The 1895 legislation against professionalism in any form could no longer touch the defectors, but instead it caught a far more distinguished player altogether. This was the Newport and Wales centre for whom many claims ring down the years as the greatest ever centre three-quarter, Arthur Gould. Gould's sin was no hole in the corner affair of a few pounds slipped into his

---

*Ibid.
**Although Rugby League is a professional game, there are no full-time professionals even today. There are also hosts of amateur rugby league players, so the 1893 verdict has hardly brought a fully professional sport in its wake.

boot, but an unwitting attempt by his many admirers to bring his illustrious career to a fitting close. In January 1897 he captained Wales for the last time, appropriately on his own ground at Rodney Parade, Newport, against England. Wales beat England for only the third time in fourteen encounters with Tom Pearson and Arthur Boucher, Gould's club mates, and Dan Jones of Aberavon all scoring tries, and W. J. Bancroft converting one for a very satisfying 14 points to 0 victory.

Gould was now thirty-two and had already officially retired, but when Newport prevailed on him to help them for one more season, the Welsh Rugby Union had been just as keen to ask him to retain the Welsh captaincy. This he did and the England international brought him an international record of 27 caps. This unique feat, allied to the immense popularity his good looks and sparkling play had earned him, was thought worthy of special notice and admirers collected together to give him a testimonial. The idea was so popular the fund quickly swelled, donations came in from all over the world, the Welsh Rugby Union themselves put in £50 and a total sum of some £600 was collected. It was decided, rather touchingly, that he should be freed from any worries that he might have, by the trustees of the fund buying the deeds of his rented house from his landlord.

The matter came to the notice of the International Board and the Rugby Union. The IB declared that any gift in money or in kind was professionalism on the part of the givers, and on the part of Gould if he accepted. That got the Welsh Rugby Union on the raw and although they were, in deference to the Board, originally prepared to withdraw their own contribution, and although Gould's first intention was to refuse the gift if it meant he would be declared a professional, a combination of administrative tactlessness at headquarters and the virulence of Welsh public opinion, changed all their minds. The Welsh Union did not withdraw their money, and at Newport on Easter Monday 1897, the Welsh President presented Gould with the title deeds of his house.

To place the affair in perspective, one should remember that two years before, W. G. Grace's admirers organised no less than three testimonials which reaped the distinguished doctor some £8,835. No one thought that that made W. G. a professional any more than his acceptance of three pigs from an admiring farmer. Similar absurdities and anomalies made the concept of amateurism untenable even in these early times.*

At least the Rugby Union, whose reaction to the presentation was to ban Gould from playing rugby (not that he wanted to any longer) and to forbid all English players and clubs from playing against him, were brought to their senses by their own members at an open vote taken at the September 1897 general meeting. A proposal that the ban was lifted 'under the exceptional circumstances of the case' was carried by a large majority. Others, particularly the Scots, were less forgiving, and when the International Board asked the Welsh RU in January 1898 to give an undertaking not to pick Gould they refused with some asperity. As a result, Scotland did not play Wales for two seasons, Ireland did not play them for one, and the England game was delayed until April. Another International series had been sabotaged by disputes.

From 1890 to 1898, Scotland could have some claim to being the strongest international force. Of the eight championships that were actually decided, they won three and shared one. In Scotland, the 'old boys' of the public school were paramount, not that they had any affection for so blatantly English a term, preferring Former Pupils, Academicals, or the suffix *'Blank-onians'*. Few clubs were openly recruited, and the tendency was for the Scottish player to go through his school and club career playing with and against the same players from boyhood to retirement. This must have had distinct advantages in team building and in instinctive understanding of colleagues in the international team, but it also had the drawback that a particular pattern of play was followed blindly.

To understand what this particular pattern was, we have to look at a typical Scottish school. H. H. Almond, the headmaster of Loretto school, gave in 1892** a graphic picture of the approach. One need not delve into the Puritan strain in the Scottish soul or the evident spiritual attractions of mortification

*For example, Fry's Chocolate advertisements appearing in 1909 carried endorsements of the product by sportsmen like Gould, Gwyn Nicholls and C. B. Fry – circumstantial evidence which could lead to an athlete being declared a professional even today.

**'Rugby in Scottish Schools' in Rev. F. Marshall *Football the Rugby Union Game* 1892 edition, pp. 51–66.

of the flesh, to see how much the philosophies of the Muscular Christians held sway in Scottish public schools. A tender infant who looked forward to a gentle introduction to the so-called happiest days of his life was in for a rude awakening. The first thing the school had to do was to make

> ... a good stand-up fight against the soft and self-indulgent ways of living in which town boys, at all events of the richer classes, are usually brought up ...

Rugby football was the medium; scholars need not apply.

> Training which would be too severe for the rapidly-growing or anaemic boy is the best possible discipline ... for the boy who prefers sitting over the fire with a book to the free air of heaven.

The incentive was always a place in one of the school's XVs:

> It has come to be understood, even by the smallest boys, that a place in any of the teams cannot usually be gained without a good deal of trouble and self-denial. Small schools also become aware that they cannot hope for football emi- nence unless they bring not only a select few but the whole mass of their boys into the fittest possible condition.

Merchiston training schedules ('... in recent years I believe the best football in the world has been played at Merchiston') are outlined, although it is made clear there was little difference between Merchiston and any other leading Scottish school. The boys were called at 7 for a ¾ mile walk or run followed by a cold bath and a rub down. Breakfast was at 8, followed by three hours of lessons from 9 to 12. From 12.30 to 1.30 on Mondays the first XV played a team of masters and old boys. At the same time on Tuesdays, the first XV coached the second XV and then spent half an hour practising their kicking and passing. On Wednesday afternoons there was a full match or a seven to ten mile cross country run over hills (2.30 to 5). On Thursdays from 12.30 to 1.30, the first XV had another hour match as per Mondays, and on Fridays from 12 to 1.30 they were given an hour's cadet corps drill followed by another half hour session of kicking and passing. Every afternoon there was forty minutes of gymnastics, and every evening for the first XV half an hour's fencing and boxing.

This kind of ferocious training undoubtedly supplied the Scottish team with an army of fit, courageous and disciplined forwards who could dribble the ball with a controlled fury, and its corollary in men who would risk a boot in the head or the ribs by falling on the ball to stop such a movement. Down to today nothing seems to rouse a Murrayfield crowd like the call of Feet! Feet! Feet! at a forward rush, or receive the same amount of applause as a headlong dive at the forwards' feet. The seductiveness of the 'feet, feet, feet' philosophy* meant that Scotland were the last to appreciate the possibilities of the handling game, reluctant to see the introduction of a fourth three-quarter, and opposed to the numbering of players' shirts for the benefit of spectators.

Contributing to E. H. D. Sewell's *Rugby Football Up to Date* as late as 1921, C. D. Stuart (winner of seven Scottish caps from 1909 to 1911) shows conclusively how much prejudice there was against newer styles of play. He is talking of the decline in Scottish forwards.

It may be argued that their object is to make the game more 'open'. This they can only do at the expense of their more honest colleagues, but one would like to ask why more 'open'? Is this great sport to be sacrificed for spectacular display? Is Rugby Football to be played for the benefit of the player, or for the entertainment of the spectator? It is first and last a game by which players gain health, exercise and courage, and to attempt to make it anything else would be fatal to its influence as a sport.

In the 1890s, no such nonsense held sway and the Scottish heroes of the day were all forwards – Mark Morrison of the Royal High School, a big, strong and fiery forward who won 23 Scottish caps from 1896 to 1904, R. G. Macmillan of London Scottish who played at international level for ten years for 21 caps, and perhaps the most famous, D. R. Bedell-Sivright, who played 22 times for his country between 1900 and 1908** and

---

*Contemporary reports and subsequent reminiscences make it clear that this was by no means a blind kick and rush affair but rather a closely controlled dribble.

**He was given credit by many perceptive observers for pioneering wing forward play before Gallaher, the New Zealander, reached these shores.

whose Muscular Christianity tended to be more Old Testament muscular than New Testament Christian. All of them had this capacity to swoop down the field shoulder to shoulder with their fellows, the ball at their toes, and waste and destruction promised for any in their path. It was an extraordinary tradition.

Ireland could not quite match this tradition but they too had their fine seasons winning the Triple Crown in 1893–4 and again in 1898–9, a feat that was to escape them again for fifty years. In Ireland too rugby was very much a game for the university man, and also something of a private dispute between forward and forward at which backs were no more than tolerated. Heart, courage and energy the Irish forwards had in abundance, but unlike the Scots they 'were immaculately innocent of training' (a description of the team they put in the field in their first ever encounter with England, when 'in the tight scrummages they could do what they liked, often shoving the Saxons the length of a cricket crease; but when the ball got loose, they were too blown to follow up').

Where the Scotsman, therefore, from a tender age, saw success at rugby as due reward for following strictly the principles of the protestant work ethic, the Irishman had a fine catholic contempt for the rehearsals and relied exclusively on the inspiration of the moment in the game itself. The Scots won more often, but an Irish win tended to be that bit more exciting.

C. V. Rooke of Dublin University, a red-haired giant who won 19 caps from 1891 to 1897 and who would have tackled an armoured car if the opposition had put one into the field, was, like Bedell-Sivright of Scotland, a pioneer of scientific wing-forward play, and with the ball at his feet a skilful and ferocious problem for a defence. And in later years, Irishmen looked to A. Tedford of Malone (23 caps 1902–8), a smaller but ultimately more skilful player than Rooke for he had handling ability too. Forty years later, a vastly experienced rugby writer* called Tedford 'the greatest of Irish forwards, the equal of the best in England, Scotland, Wales or New Zealand'. Praise indeed.

The pleasure in reading now of the fighting spirit of the Scottish and Irish forwards of the 1890s and the early 1900s, and certainly they wrote themselves into the annals of the game, has to be tinged with regret that neither country produced backs

*W. J. Townsend Collins in *Rugby Recollections* 1948.

to match them. It may have been that the natural talent was not there anyway, but somehow one feels that the climate of opinion was not right to encourage such a development. The Scots could point to the talents of J. G. Gillespie or A. B. Timms, the Irish to Louis Magee or Basil Maclear*, yet somehow these names have not retained the magic that is still afforded the host of halves and three-quarters who donned the scarlet jersey of Wales.

From about 1900 to 1911, Wales were supreme at rugby football. They won the International Championship in 1900, 1902, 1905, 1906 (when they tied with Ireland), 1908, 1909 and 1911 and they won the mythical but gratifying Triple Crown in every one of those years except 1906. Seven championships and six Triple Crowns was the major achievement in Edwardian rugby.

It has often been said since that this golden period for Welsh rugby came because of the talented backs which the country could draw on. Certainly the reputation of a three-quarter line composed of Teddy Morgan, Rhys Gabe, E. Gwyn Nicholls and Willie Llewellyn ('perhaps the most illustrious in Welsh rugby history' J. B. G. Thomas has said) has scarcely diminished in the intervening years, but the view is to conceal another truth – that they would not have played as they did if they had not been heirs to a quite different rugby tradition to that of Scotland, Ireland and England.

In an article he wrote in October 1906,** Arthur Gould put the current Welsh success down to 'the elevation of team combination to a fine art', and to the willingness of the whole team to recognise that because attacks could best be launched by three-quarters it was best for a team to play to its backs. Completely contrary to the Irish and Scottish forward theories, and particularly to the views of Englishmen like Arthur Budd as this idea was, Gould argued that because of the skill in passing to create scoring opportunities – 'The world of rugby football has never seen anything to equal the swiftness and accuracy of Welsh passing' – it was not a matter of genius at work, but a matter of

---

*"No Irish centre was ever so extravagantly praised . . . he certainly was not the equal of Sam Lee who preceded him, or of G. V. Stephenson who followed . . . " was what Townsend Collins thought.

**In *C. B. Fry's Magazine*.

achieving excellent results 'with *comparatively ordinary material*' (Gould's italics).

Of course one's first reaction is to say that if Nicholls and company were ordinary material, we would sure like to see some about now, but there is circumstantial evidence to suggest that the dependence on the four is not quite as heavy as one would think. Teddy Morgan played his last game for Wales in 1908,* Gabe his last in 1908, Nicholls his last in 1907 (and that against South Africa), and Willie Llewellyn his last in 1906.** And yet Welsh supremacy continued with the 1908, 1909 and 1911 Championships and the Triple Crowns that went with them.

After the illustrious quartet, Wales had J. P. Jones*** of Newport and Pontypool (a classic centre, a hard and straight runner with a controlled swerve and accurate scoring pass who got his first cap in 1909 and his last in 1921), W. J. Trew of Swansea (29 caps from 1900 to 1913, captain of Wales for more victories, twelve, than any player before or since,**** and a superlative player at centre, wing or outside-half), W. J. Spiller of Cardiff (10 caps from 1907 to 1911, a man who developed a devastating side-step and who scored 17 tries for Wales in just 17 matches – compared with Llewellyn's 16 in 20), and Reggie Gibbs of Cardiff (16 caps from 1907 to 1911, *seventeen* tries in just 16 appearances compared with Morgan's 14 in 16, and who popped over three conversions as well).

I am not concerned to try to take anything away from Nicholls and company, their deeds and their reputations speak for themselves. But one must record the curious fact that even in Welsh rugby circles, Trew and especially Messrs Jones, Spiller and Gibbs are rarely afforded the honour they would seem to have earned. If they had not that indefinable touch of genius, and that is subjective and arguable, they were certainly pretty effective. What is more important to my mind is that if we give too much attention to the quartet, we will miss the full im-

*Only against France, his last full international season was in 1906, and he played but once (against South Africa) in 1907.

**Against the All Blacks – his last full season for Wales was in 1905.

***Usually called 'Ponty' to distinguish him from J. P. 'Tuan' Jones also of Pontypool.

****By way of comparison, two post-war captaincy records read: Clive Rowlands 6 victories, 14 matches; John Gwilliam 9 victories, 13 matches.

portance of what the Welsh did to, and for, Edwardian rugby.

The crucial difference between English, Scottish and Irish rugby on the one hand and rugby in Wales on the other, is that in Wales, just as soccer was in Scotland, rugby was the game of the masses rather than of the classes. Because they were not taught how to play at school, and because there were no un-written laws that stifled individual enterprise they developed their own tactics. We have already seen how the soccer-playing Scots were not bounded by the ubiquitous desire of the English to put their heads down and dribble towards goal. In the same way, the Welsh were not indoctrinated with the idea that rugby was wholly about raw courage displayed in the ever present scrummages.

It may well be, although conclusive proof would be very difficult to find because of the unavailability of statistics, that many of the soccer-playing Scots and the rugby-playing Welsh were smaller, frailer men than their English contemporaries, and they had to do with skill and wit what the Englishmen could do with superior weight and brawn. Mental attitudes were different too — where the English saw a defence as something to be ploughed *through,* the Welsh and the Scots, unmindful of the theory that this was the 'manly' way to play, chose to find their way *around* defences.

Much of the Welsh success in that first decade of the twentieth century can surely be traced to the activities of the major Welsh clubs in the preceding years. As rugby itself developed, and twenty a side was succeeded by fifteen a side, there was for some time confusion as to the best disposition of forces. The first fifteen a side international between England and Ireland in February 1877 was played between sets of eight forwards, three full-backs, two three-quarters and two half-backs apiece. In 1881, England v Scotland was played between ten forwards and five backs, as indeed it was in 1882, although Scotland had experimented with three three-quarters against Ireland in 1881 and lost by a goal to a try.

Out of this confusion grew a convention that the best formula was nine forwards, two half-backs, three three-quarters and one full-back. One of the two full-backs having been found super-flous, most sides settled for putting the extra man into the for-wards where the action generally was.

This did not apply at Cardiff. Out of a happy accident in February 1883, Cardiff found themselves with an Englishman, F. E. Hancock, who though originally a forward, had proved his worth in the three-quarter line. Reluctant to dispense with either his services or those of their regular three-quarters, they played four three-quarters against Gloucester, and although they only achieved a draw, the system had its evident advantages. Under Hancock's direction, the club polished the new formula so successfully over the next few seasons that in January 1886, Wales* brought Hancock in as captain against Scotland and fielded four three-quarters.

The nine-strong Scottish pack tore through the Welsh eight with gusto and despite a panic reaction whereby the Welsh full-back was sent into the forwards, and Gould was dropped back from the centre to full-back, Scotland ran out winners by two goals and a try to nil. Unfairly, the system was blamed rather than its exponents, and it was only in December 1888 against the Maori touring team that the experiment was repeated, and became obligatory thereafter. It was Cardiff's unique legacy to Welsh football.

Over at Newport, the running talents of Arthur Gould were sufficient to carry the three three-quarter system, but that was possible because of the tremendous share of the ball that successive packs of Newport forwards were able to win for him. (Gould was later converted to the 'four' system and the latter part of his international career was spent with a partner in the centre culminating in three matches in which he and Gwyn Nicholls played in tandem). Newport were unbeaten in 1891–2, winning 29 games and drawing 4, meanwhile scoring 72 goals and 96 tries to 3 goals and 5 tries; lost only 3 matches in 1892–3, only 3 again in 1893–4, and a bare one in 1894–5.

This was not a matter of Newport happening to find great forwards, but rather developing them, for according to S. M. J. Woods,** the success was built in evening sessions in the gymnasium working on general fitness and scrummaging techniques alike. From Newport therefore Wales learned that the best combination of backs would be useless unless a set of what became known as 'big Rhondda forwards' could be found to at least

*National qualifications were never too rigid then.
**Woods won 13 English caps between 1890 and 1895.

contain English, Irish and Scottish packs. By the end of the 1890s Wales found the right kind of forwards and in 1900 followed a 13–3 victory over England with a 12–3 win over Scotland. Said Mark Morrison, the Scottish captain, 'the Welsh forwards completely over-ran us'. The road to a decade of success was open.

Swansea, the other great club team of the period, contributed two things as well. One was a full-blooded commitment to attack. (For three years the club's playing record was as follows:

1900 P–32 W–31 L–1 D–0 Points For–586 Against–57
1901 P–28 W–24 L–2 D–2 Points For–400 Against–46
1902 P–29 W–21 L–3 D–5 Points For–361 Against–67

Full-back W. J. Bancroft was once asked by a new Swansea recruit, 'How do we defend?' and got the pithy answer, 'I can't remember, all the games I've played, we've only attacked!).

Swansea's other legacy came from the James brothers, half-backs who showed conclusively that diminutive stature was no drawback in rugby if it came along with the ability to dodge, swerve, dummy, pass and inter-pass until the opposing forwards were left grasping thin air and despairing of ever finding out where the ball would be next. Invented by them, developed by Llewellyn Lloyd of Newport, Dicky Owen of Swansea, Percy Bush of Cardiff, Tommy Vile of Newport and Billy Trew when he had the time, Welsh half-back play became synonymous with wit and trickery and the foundations were laid for a tradition that has continued ever since. It also provided the vital link between forwards and backs that was to make the following ten year period of Welsh rugby a triumph, not for four men in particular, but for team rugby and for a unique combination of Swansea, Cardiff and Newport virtues.

Weakened by the schism of 1895 and reluctant to learn from the Welsh example, England stayed in the rugby doldrums until the eve of the First World War. The *Daily Telegraph* rugby correspondent, Major Philip Trevor, put it accurately and topically in 1902:

... in two very different fields many of the great in the land are as blind to the efficacy of Welsh tactics as they are to the efficacy of Boer tactics.

It was not that England did not have rugby talent available; according to A. J. Gould they were plagued by selection blunders. He was firmly of the opinion, and it has the ring of truth, that in the Western and South Western parts of England, clubs *'where the game is taken seriously'* (my italics), remained dangerous rivals to the Welsh clubs.

Major Trevor returned to the theme in 1905. He pointed to the weakness of the fixture list of the average English first class club, to the geographical difficulties of selection as opposed to Wales where three counties produced the national team and where it was possible 'to guess twelve of the fifteen of the Wales team in advance', and to the innate conservatism of the English who were reluctant to learn from the Welsh back play, as the Welsh had learned from English forward play.

When England did eventually learn some of the lessons, she shared the championship with Ireland in 1912, and won the Triple Crown in 1913 and 1914. The fruits must have been that much sweeter for the self-denial of the previous decade. On January 20th 1912 at Twickenham, Adrian Stoop, the Oxford University English outside half and captain, led his men out before the game for a team photograph. A Welsh supporter threw a leek at him which Stoop picked up and solemnly buried in the Twickenham turf. With that symbolic act, Welsh domination came to an end.

England rising like a phoenix from the ashes owed her new eminence primarily to the contribution of one club, the illustrious Harlequins. The club captaincy was taken over in 1905 by Adrian Stoop, and under him the Quins were to achieve new heights and a lasting reputation for back play. Stoop recruited, planned and coached his players in his belief in attacking rugby which never allowed opponents to regroup after an unnecessary touch-kick. His backs were to run with the ball, and this they did to such effect that between 1905 and 1911 ten Harlequin backs were capped for England. The first season the club played at Twickenham (the new ground was first used on October 2nd, 1909 for a Harlequins home game against Richmond) they scored 541 points in 24 matches – an average of over 20 points a game.

Stoop, the master strategist, his two most famous protégés, J. G. Birkett, a strapping, hard-running centre and Ronald Poulton (later Poulton-Palmer) a graceful and elusive runner, plus Stoop's England successor at outside-half, W. J. A. Davies of the Navy (Davies' most famous partner C. A. Kershaw did not play for England until after the First World War), might be said to have restored England's morale and reputation.

Poulton-Palmer was an inspired genius if contemporary accounts are to be believed. He once went through an entire South African defence swerving in and out down one wing to place the ball under the posts at his leisure. He scored five tries on his first appearance in the 1909 Varsity match, and 20 tries in 17 appearances for England. He also had a conventional public school and University background, and a private income of £20,000 per annum but, as the brilliant unorthodoxy of his rugby suggests, he was not bound by the ethics, conventions and prejudices common amongst his colleagues. When he heard that the RFU were to conduct an enquiry into rumours of 'broken-time' payments being made in some Devonshire rugby clubs, he wrote a heartfelt and damning letter to *The Sportsman* in 1913.

> If it is the desire of the RFU committee practically to limit the game to players who learn it at the Public Schools, and in the Services and Universities, such a finding is reasonable. But I cannot believe such is their desire. Was not this, then, the opportunity to put the game on an immovable basis among all classes of the community . . . such an action as the Rugby Union Committee have taken will do much to prevent the expansion of the Rugby game, and so reduce the value to England of the most democratic of sports . . .

Killed in action in the War and buried in a war grave in Belgium, Poulton-Palmer was, in more than one sense, a person English rugby could ill afford to lose.

We have now seen some of the individual contributions each home country made to the way rugby was played for the rise of French rugby was yet in the future. Although France played against England first in 1905–6, against Wales first in 1907–8, against Ireland first in 1908–9 and against Scotland first in 1909–10, she was not looked on as providing serious opposition. Admittedly, France scraped home 16–15 against Scotland in 1911 but this did not go far to wipe out the impression of Gallic incompetence caused by slaughters like the 1907 English victory 41–13, or the Welsh 47–5 win in Paris in 1909.

It is to the Empire, not to Europe that we must look for other major influences on the game. Just before our period opens, a Maori tour of Britain was reciprocated by a private venture to New Zealand and Australia. Travelling under the manager A. E. Stoddart, the cricketer, and without the blessing of the Rugby Union who considered it a purely speculative financial operation to line the pockets of two professional cricketers (Alfred Shaw and Arthur Shrewsbury) and their friends, the tour got off to a bad start with a Halifax forward J. P. Clowes being declared a professional for daring to accept free boots from a sports outfitters. That he could not afford them himself was no excuse. During the tour, R. L. Seddon, the captain, was drowned in a bathing accident and Stoddart himself took over the captaincy. The playing record was impressive – P–35* W–27 D–6 L–2 Points For–300 Against–101 – but no internationals were played. The two losses (to Auckland and to Taranaki Clubs) were narrow ones. Probably the most significant fact historically speaking is that the team showed New Zealand players that heeling the ball at a scrummage did not place one's own men offside – in view of the way New Zealand rugby progressed thereafter in a miraculously short time, British interests might have been better served if the tourists had perpetuated the misconception.

The first tour to be blessed with official favour was in 1891 to South Africa. Under W. E. Maclagan of Edinburgh Academicals and Scotland, twenty-one English and Scottish players, nearly half of them from Cambridge University, played nineteen fixtures and won the lot, conceding but one goal on the entire tour.

South Africa were also hosts to the 1896 venture, this time a party composed of Englishmen and Irishmen under J. Hammond, a Cambridge Blue but a player who was never capped. Again it was one way traffic over South African territory and goal-lines, and only the final match of the tour was lost (the Third and final Test against South Africa by a converted try to nil). There seemed no danger that the Springboks might yet become a threat to British rugby.

*This does not include another 19 they played under Australian rules – a pointer to the casual nature of the proceedings.

In 1899, a party, less than half of them internationals but including one Welshman (Gwyn Nicholls), three Irishmen, three Scots and fourteen Englishmen, went off to the southern hemisphere for 21 matches (winning 18 and losing 3) but they only visited Australia, not New Zealand. That English rugby had declined since the famous split is more obviously shown by the composition of the party that went next to South Africa in 1903 under Mark Morrison of Scotland. The eight Englishmen were in a minority, for of the rest of the twenty-one players one was Welsh, seven Scottish and five Irish. And that seven year gap had done much for South African rugby, as is clear from the playing record. This time the British team won only eleven matches, drew three and lost eight. At Test level, they could not win one match and after 10–10 and 0–0 draws, lost the Third Test 0–8, and the series with it. The solitary Welshman, R. T. Skrimshire of Newport, was the one star of the back division, but the South Africans had Loubser on the right-wing and Krige in the centre to feed him. It was quite a partnership, as British crowds were able to testify a few years later.

The following year, 1904, one of the forwards in Morrison's party, D. R. Bedell-Sivright took a British team to Australia and New Zealand. The major part of the tour was 14 matches in Australia, including three tests, but the team romped through those undefeated. With Gabe, Llewellyn and Morgan in the three-quarter line and Percy Bush of Cardiff and Tommy Vile of Newport as half-backs, it did not lack for talent outside the scrum, but where the largely uncapped club and county forwards held their own in Australia, they were over-matched in the five matches in New Zealand, losing to Auckland 0–13 and to New Zealand 3–9 in the only test. But because these matches took place thousands of miles away from Great Britain, not much attention was paid. Consequently the First All Blacks who came here in 1905–6 were a revelation – the Edwardians had their virtues, but awareness that there were others in the world beside themselves was not one of them.

Even if there had been no All Black tour in 1905–6 (which we will come to in a moment), the English and Welsh players who in 1908 toured Australia (9 fixtures, no tests) and New Zealand (17 fixtures, 3 tests), could have told any who doubted that New Zealand rugby had not been standing still in the last decade and a half. On the contrary, New Zealand could now put men into the field capable of absorbing the best the opposition could throw at them and then steam-rollering them into the ground. The Anglo-Welsh hung on for a 3–3 draw in the Second Test, in which New Zealand fielded a Second XV, but that was the minutest of fig-leaves to cover the nakedness of their thinking displayed for all the rugby world to see in the losses of 5–32 in the First Test and 0–29 in the Third.

Similar woeful tales could be told of the last Edwardian venture abroad, the 1910 tour to South Africa. The obliging opposition who had looked, wondered and applauded as Maclagen's men achieved their 1891 hundred per cent record, had mysteriously undergone a metamorphosis in the intervening nineteen years. Not only had they caught up to British methods, they had left them behind in a particularly ungrateful fashion. They now proceeded to return the lesson with interest. C. H. Pillman of Blackheath and England, a genius in constructive and destructive wing-forward play, distinguished himself to such an extent that he has been credited as being the ancestor of most South African number 8's, but most of his colleagues were pupils rather than masters. They lost a third of their 24 matches, and two of those were Tests. They won a Second Test 8–3 but lost the First 10–14 and the deciding Third by a resounding 5–21.

In other words, New Zealand and South Africa, even if they had not sent teams to Britain before the First World War, had given plenty of signs that, for the next half-century and more, supremacy would be decided between themselves, and that unless the birthplace of the game came up with new ideas, we were condemned to second-class citizenship in world rugby. With a combination of blissful ignorance and assumed superiority, akin to that of a prop forward pushing vainly in a scrum with little but a vacuum and a scrum cap to keep his ears apart, British rugby went haphazardly on its merry but ineffective way until the nineteen seventies.

What made this insularity particularly irritating is that whereas in association football there was little enough opportunity for an Edwardian to see what other countries were doing, in rugby there was every chance. Three major tours to Britain, one from New Zealand and two from South Africa, in 1905–6, 1906–7, and 1912–13, took place. All three wrote their message large that British was not always best, but in each case, the Edwardians chose not to read the message.

In large black (and Black!) letters, the stop press section of some London evening papers at the start of the 1905–6 season carried a result from down in Devonshire. It read: Devon 4 pts, All Blacks 55 pts. Some readers failed to see it, some optimists dismissed it as a clear case of transposition of Devon 55 pts, All Blacks (whoever they might be) 4 pts, and a few pessimists thought All Blacks 5 pts, Devon 4 pts was what had been intended. Over the next few weeks, the accuracy of London compositors had been vindicated as an All Black tide swept over English rugby. After Devon, the New Zealand party played Cornwall, Bristol, Northampton, Leicester, Middlesex, Durham and West Hartlepool. The scores were 41–0, 41–0, 32–0, 28–0, 34–0, 16–3, 63–0 all in favour of the New Zealanders. Those sorts of scores took a great deal of explaining away.

Attempts were made. The New Zealand styles and tactics were analysed in great length, but probably because the writers were looking for excuses rather than reasons, the undoubted facts that the All Blacks had strength, speed, skill, weight and a team understanding far superior of their opponents, and that their rugby thinking was some light years ahead of most, were rarely mentioned. Rather, they and particularly their captain Gallaher, were criticised for blatant obstruction.

That Gallaher's role was undoubtedly contrary to both the spirit and letter of the laws of the game cannot seriously be questioned. The method was this. Instead of the conventional packing down of eight forwards in 3–2–3 formation at set scrummages, the All Blacks went down 2–3–2 and the eighth forward Gallaher stood outside the scrum. As soon as the scrum was down, Gallaher instead of the scrum half put the ball in. It was hooked in the front row and shot back between the legs of the lock in the middle of the second row, to be picked up by the scrum half waiting at the base of the scrum (he did not have to run around first as Gallaher had done half of his work for him). The two men in the back row packed obligingly wide with a convenient gap between them for the passage of the ball, yet they could easily tap the ball back to the lock if the scrum half did not want to receive it yet. The scrum half usually wanted to receive it all right, for not only did he get the ball faster than any of the British halves, he had Gallaher standing alongside him to prevent any of the opposition collaring him while he made up his mind what to do with it. The critics saw this piece of obstruction clearly enough, but what few of them saw was seven forwards who could hold eight comfortably because each man had a specific job to do in the scrum. British forwards went down 3–2–3 – but that usually meant the front three were merely the first three on the scene, for scrums were formed like bus queues on a first up, first down principle.

While the observers quibbled about the ethics of Gallaher's role and neglected the lessons implicit in the speedy backing up the New Zealanders gave each other, the spate of victories continued.

Scotland, who lost 12–7, after leading for most of the game, were not the most gracious of hosts. At first they refused to stage the match, then decided to do so without awarding caps to the Scottish players. They failed to cover the pitch, which was frozen solid, and the game took place because Gallaher was not the obstructionist off the field he was on it. The Scottish players found it beneath their dignity to mix socially with rough colonials (the match was not always played in the best spirit) and after the game the Scottish Rugby Union actually insisted that the match ball kept by the All Blacks as a souvenir of their first international on British soil should be returned. The New Zealanders had the last laugh because their share of the gate from the match came to £17,000, but the Scots kept up a campaign against them for another four years, demanding to see a full financial statement of the tour from the Rugby Union. This was supplied a year after it had been requested and was used as evidence by the Scots to break off relations with the Rugby Union in January 1909 and to cancel the Calcutta Cup match of that season (a healing of the breach later meant the match was played after all) on the dubious basis that the Rugby Union, by giving the 1906 New Zealanders and the 1909 Australians a 3s a day allowance per player, 'was encouraging professionalism'.*

---

*Resentments lingered long afterwards and Scotland refused any fixtures with the Second All-Blacks in 1924. They conveniently forgot that players on the 1904 British tour to Australia and New Zealand, *captained by a Scotsman*, had been paid 2s a day 'wine money'.

Ireland were the next to go down to New Zealand, respectably but never with a chance of winning, 15–0, and then the tourists were back in England for another 15–0 win over the national XV. As the points were all from unconverted tries, they were relatively untroubled. Pausing only to put 18 points on Cheltenham, 34 on Cheshire and 40 on Yorkshire, the party came to Wales. Their record was now 27 matches, 27 wins and a colossal 801 points for to a mere 21 against.

The Welsh, riding high in domestic rugby, had prepared well.* In answer to Gallaher's ploy, they withdrew Cliff Pritchard from the pack and played seven forwards in the scrum. Pritchard harried when New Zealand won the ball and operated as a dummy outside-half when Wales heeled and Dicky Owen, the Weslsh scrum-half, had the ball. The only score of the match came from the carefully planned use of Pritchard's roving commission. Owen got the ball, Bush at outside half ran to the right and Owen dummied a pass to him only to sling a reverse pass to Pritchard on the left of the scrum. Pritchard drew a man and passed to Gabe, Gabe did the same and passed to Morgan who had just enough room to round Gillett and touch down in the corner.

Possession from the scrum was won for this move, and often in the match, by the Welsh forwards cancelling out the hooking skill of the two All-Black front-row men. This they did by putting two men down in the front row, but keeping two men out until they knew which side the ball would be put in. Once this was clear, and here referee Dallas sometimes helped by insisting that Gallaher put the ball in from the blind-side, a third man was added on that side to give them a permanent loose-head. Owen, when he was allowed to, also threw the ball in hard against the New Zealand legs for Wales to hook the rebound!

For another fifty minutes of fierce tension and even fiercer tackling, battle raged, but New Zealand failed to score . . . or did they? For the last seventy years, New Zealanders have said they did, Welshmen have said no. No sporting argument has been pursued with greater vigour. What happened was this. Wallace, New Zealand's magnificent winger, gathered an ill-directed kick

---

*Llewellyn, Morgan, Bush, Harding and Gabe of the Welsh team had been to New Zealand on tour.

from a line-out and cut diagonally into the centre of the field. Confronted with Nicholls and Gabe on the half-way line, he side-stepped and went between them. Just before he could reach the Welsh 25, Winfield, the Welsh full back, came at him, obviously determined not to take a dummy. Before Wallace could be downed, and the ball lost, Bob Deans was up on his left calling for the ball. The pass was given and taken, and as Winfield tackled Wallace, Deans ran on for the Welsh line. He got there with the recovered Gabe breathing down his neck, Morgan from the Welsh left wing using his speed to cut him off and Cliff Pritchard in hot pursuit. Either Gabe or Morgan tackled him on the Welsh line or both. (Both Gabe and Morgan claimed later to have done so).

Neither side would dispute this sequence of events, but did Deans put the ball down before the line, on the line (which would be a try) or over it? By the time referee Dallas got to the spot, the ball and Deans were short of the line and he disallowed the score. Deans was adamant that he had scored for the rest of his life. Dallas was adamant that he had not.

Writing in 1954, Gabe said this. 'When I brought him down I thought that he had (scored), but when I found him struggling I sensed that he had not, and I, with Cliff Pritchard, pulled him back' and on a radio discussion in 1939, he said 'I certainly ought to know. It was I who tackled Deans'. Rather nearer to the event, Morgan wrote in 1921, but less often quoted:

... The late R. G. Deans ... in the opinion of several of the players including myself, and the Welsh touch-judge, Ack Llewellyn, scored that oft-quoted try against Wales in December 1905 at Cardiff. How it happened I cannot exactly tell you, but it was I who tackled him to prevent him running behind. As I tackled him (a few yards outside) *I distinctly saw the white goal-line underneath me,* and yet, when I got up off Deans' legs, he was holding on to the ball (with two others of our side) which was grounded about a foot outside the line. Deans was claiming a try in no uncertain voice. Dallas, the referee, came running up from the Grand Stand side, and had not seen what had happened after the tackle. (My italics)

And in 1924, at a post match dinner, Morgan wrote a message to Wallace on Cliff Porter's* menu card. It said, 'Deans *did* score at Cardiff'. To my mind, Morgan's words, particularly those I have italicised, have the ring of authentic recollection about them. Back in 1905, Deans sent a post-match telegram to the *Daily Mail*......

GROUNDED BALL SIX INCHES OVER LINE SOME OF WELSH PLAYERS ADMIT TRY HUNTER AND GLASGOW CAN CONFIRM WAS PULLED BACK BEFORE REFEREE ARRIVED. DEANS.

and the rugby correspondent of *The Sportsman* was equally adamant:

I was within six yards of the spot when the New Zealanders scored the disallowed try. It was the unanimous verdict of a goodly number of Welsh supporters next to me, and also my own, that no fairer try has been scored on the football field.

On balance, my objectivity overcoming my Welsh patriotism, the evidence does suggest the score was valid. Gabe, who tackled Deans just before or just after Morgan, could not have been in the best position to see the line by his own admission, and he and Pritchard were not there to adjudicate but to prevent a score if humanly possible. Deans would hardly be likely to lie prone if he had scored by so narrow a margin but would surely try to move forward *in case* he was pulled back. They in their turn, could hardly do other than pull him back *in case* he was not yet there. In the absence of the referee, and without any attempt at dishonesty by either side, a tug of war was inevitable and in that three were bound to beat one. One sympathises with the All Blacks in losing their unbeaten record in so unsatisfactory a fashion, but if their backing-up had been up to their own high standards, the tug of war would have been three against three at least and they could have held Deans' *status quo*.

Having failed to beat Wales, the party looked more vulnerable for their remaining club matches in Wales. Newport ran them to 6–3, Swansea to 4–3 and Cardiff, thanks to an extraordinary slip by Percy Bush who presented them with a try, lost only

*Cliff Porter was the captain of the Second All-Blacks of 1924.

10–8, so perhaps the disallowed Deans' score was justice of the poetic kind if not technically sound.

The playing record of Paul Roos's First Springboks in Britain of 1906–7 is almost as impressive as that of Gallaher's men – P–29 W–26 L–2 D–1, the draw against England (3–3) and the two losses, against Scotland (0–6) and against Cardiff (0–17), all being sustained when the pitches had turned into muddy quagmires. They packed down more conventionally than New Zealand as 3–3–2, and they brought to Britain, not so much new technical ideas, as a living demonstration of how effective British styles could be if they were played by men prepared to use physique, speed and determination to win the ball and to run straight at the opposition. Three-quarters like Loubser, Morkel and Krige set this sort of tradition for running through rather than around tackles for the Gainsfords of the future, and very effective it was too. Behind the threes, the 1906–7 'Boks had full back Marsberg, who became legendary for sheer recklessness in tackling, saving and running regardless of how many opposition forwards came at him, a reputation which survived a boot in the head in a last minute dive at the feet of the Scottish forwards. Scotland's win was earned by their forwards' foot rushes and dribbles and a refusal to allow the South African threes room to work up speed. As novelist A. G. Hales colourfully suggested, a Springbok back would

> . . . work hands and arms like a deaf mute signalling for a fire escape. The next moment a bony shoulder would connect with his ribs, and he would be making more marks on Scottish soil than Robert Burns on Scottish history.

The South Africans learned from the experience, and won a ferocious struggle against Ireland, getting to half-time 12–3 up and the game all over but the shouting only for the Irish forwards to reach heights of inspiration to draw it at 12–12, but getting a try through Stegman to decide it at 15–12.

Wales, encouraged by the closeness of these two internationals, came confidently to Swansea, but they found the South Africans had counters to every one of their ploys. The Springboks, who had lost most of the set scrum possession to Glamorgan and Newport as the Welshmen used the perpetual loose-head tactic, this time calmly moved another man up from the back-row and

115

went down 4–3–1, to counter it.* And the crosskicks from the backs, for which the Welsh forwards preferred to wait rather than run in support (a move which had often produced tries), never came because the South African threes were so quickly on their men. For all the difficulty both sides had putting the ball into the scrum (not surprisingly in view of the loose-head struggles) to the extent that Jones the referee put it in twice himself, South Africa never looked like losing and duly won 11–0. The Welsh nation had to settle for the consolation that for the Cardiff club, Nicholls and Bush were on song and defied the mud to play a handling game that brought them a 17–0 victory.**

By their win, Cardiff set another tradition, that the top Welsh clubs could be expected to present at least as difficult a task for touring sides as the Wales team. The 1908–9 Australians under H. M. Moran lost 3–8 to Llanelli ('Who-oo beat the Wall-a-bies but Good Old Sospan Fach?'), 0–6 to Swansea, and 8–24 to Cardiff. And the 1912–13 Springboks lost 3–9 to Newport and 0–3 to Swansea. The tradition has still to die.

The 1908–9 Australians left no great legacy to rugby but several aspects of their tour are illuminating of contemporary attitudes. Rugby in Australia, rather as in Wales, having a class-less character, many of the tourists on and off the field were made to feel second-class citizens, an implied status which the Australians rightly and bitterly resented. Because they were made a 3s a day allowance, they were given no fixtures in Scotland. Because problems of interpretation as to what was and what was not acceptable on the field were not settled off the field (due, said their captain, to lack of sympathy and arrogance by the English authorities) some of their members took to fisticuffs on the field and men were ordered off at Oxford, Cardiff and Swansea. To add to their discomfiture (for many of the party it

---

*The fighting for the loose-head invented by Wales for the All Blacks game was widely copied and reached its ultimate and inevitable absurdity in 1912 at a County Championship semi-final between Devon and East Midlands when both sides tried it in turn until some scrums were composed of two eight-man front rows! Moving with the speed of a snail, it was another decade before the International Board ruled in 1922 that only three men would be allowed in the front row.

**Cardiff, unlike the visitors, re-studded their players' boots when they saw the ground condition.

turned into an anti-British feeling so deeply felt that less than a quarter of them were prepared to serve for the Allies in the First World War) they were expected to mimic the All Blacks' famous haka and perform a most unauthentic aboriginal war-cry. In Moran's words 'we performed shamefacedly some grotesque antics before crowds that were not interested in the indifferent show' after which they were glad to bury their faces in the first scrum. When he reflected on the tour thirty years later, he thought one of his major achievements was in getting his men from Australia and half round the world and back in five months without one of them catching venereal disease – that they took home an Olympic gold medal each for beating Cornwall in the Rugby Final at the 1908 Olympic Games did not seem to count.

The Second Springboks came four seasons later in 1912–13, but although some of the names had changed, the tactics had but little. Apart from Newport and Swansea, only London won themselves a Springbok's head as a souvenir. Krige in the centre and Dobbin at scrum half took up where they had left off on the previous visit, and the home country sides went down with regularity before them. Scotland lost 16–0, Ireland 38–0, Wales 3–0, England 9–3, and France 38–5. It was the final proof, if any were needed, that despite the massive contribution Britain had made to rugby football, its future for a long time to come would be decided not by the old masters but by the fast-learning pupils who had since superseded them.

CHAPTER FOUR

The Golden Age of Cricket?

If any Englishman who has ever held a bat or turned an arm at cricket is asked to describe the period in the sport lasting from about 1890 to the outbreak of World War One in 1914, the odds are heavily in favour of his defining it as the Golden Age of Cricket. In 1890 cricket was the national game. By 1914 it had been overtaken by football, yet a mystique has surrounded the game ever since the era was so swiftly and mercilessly cut off by the outbreak of hostilities, that mental images of Edwardian England seem almost incomplete unless somewhere in the background white-flannelled men run to and fro, or just off-stage, the sound of willow on leather and polite applause filters through the noise in the foreground of the tinkling tea-cups and the horses' hoofs.

Major Bowen's irreproachable scholarship* has led him to confirm that there were major *cricketing* (as opposed to romantic and nostalgic) reasons for calling the period not just *a* Golden Age but *the* Golden Age of cricket. He has pointed to the way that cricket became organised centrally, how county and test cricket took modern form, how the game grew not only in the Empire but in Philadelphia and elsewhere, how League cricket developed seriously, how the laws were modernised, and, not least, how the period saw more high individual scores than ever before or since. All these are undoubted facts, and they must receive their true weight in any assessment of Edwardian cricket.

It is not however of these facts that our Englishman is usually thinking when he repeats the tag 'golden'. He is thinking more in terms of aesthetics, of style, of élan, of that indefinable spirit of the carefree and the glorious, and above all, of those

*In *Cricket*; *a history* 1970.

118

kinds of qualities displayed by top-class batsmen. Again I must quote Major Bowen;

> ... it was an age when cricket could *seem* to have reached a degree of perfection, the age from which everything has fallen away since, just as it has politically and socially (or at least from the standpoint of a great many people: and if there are many others who disagree and who would have hated to have lived in that period, many of them in turn, would have much rather played *and* watched cricket then than now).

He is much too careful and honest an historian to ignore the fact that the 'degree of perfection' was bound up inextricably with what sort of society this form of cricket was representing. Elsewhere he says, again with the acute perception that makes his book perhaps the finest work ever written on cricket, this:

> We are still very much captives of that period generally and still liable to look at it romantically: maybe in fifty years time, there will come others who will persuade themselves and others that it was a period of black iniquity disguised from the general view by highly painted and gilded lath and plaster work.

I have no intention of seeking to prove (for such a conclusion would be as false as its antithesis that all was golden) that Edwardian England was a period of black iniquity, but I would strongly deny that it is an age from which everything has fallen away politically and socially. On the contrary, if the relative decline of cricket (Major Bowen skilfully traces its downward path in tandem with Imperialism itself) was the sacrifice that had to be made for the twentieth century advance of the common man on every social, economic and political front, then that sacrifice was well worthwhile. And I say that although I love the game deeply, and although Major Bowen is probably right, I would have preferred to play and watch the game then.

I have stressed Major Bowen's accuracy and consistency, not only because they shine through every page of his book, but because they are not the foremost qualities shown by the one man who above all others, has coloured our way of thinking about Edwardian cricket. I refer, of course, to Sir Neville Cardus.

In book after book, in article after article, Sir Neville has told and retold for subsequent generations, of the great matches and the giant personalities who dominated that lost world of cricket before 1914. Few writers, let alone sports writers, have ever had so magical an ability to conjure such a profusion of metaphor and imagery, or the knack of creating mental pictures at once so powerful and so apt. No one, with the merest touch of poetry in his soul can resist a small thrill of pleasure at reading and re-reading some of his most typical allusions. Spooner and Maclaren – 'the eagle and the flashing swallow'; Spofforth and W. G. Grace – 'the forked lightning threatening the great oak'; Spofforth again – 'a killing, chilling wind fit to freeze our grass and dry up nature in our soil'; Macartney – 'his every innings was a *scherzo* – in a battle symphony . . . out of his bat's end shot the lightning that works havoc'; Ranjitsinhji – 'dark, stealthy magic'; Maclaren at the wicket – 'like reading prose in Gibbon'. Leaving aside the obvious debt to Shakespeare and the Romantic poets – for example, the last phrase about Maclaren owes not a little to Coleridge's description of Kean's acting ('like reading Shakespeare by flashes of lightning') – the image he conjures linger on in the mind thereafter. They are meant to, and to try to redress the balance by reference to literal, not literary, truth looks dull and prosaic by comparison – if *every* Macartney innings was a *scherzo,* his occasional ducks must have been whole movements composed of a semi-breve rest.

My point is that in the face of such graphic pictures from the past, how can any mortal man fail to appear a pale imitation? A Sobers may hit six sixes in an over and still look small beer compared with Jessop. But, is it really compared with Jessop, or with a poetic image that the name of Jessop has come to represent?

In 1930, Sir Neville criticised the then current England XI for their failure to measure up to the men of Edwardian times. He said that they would be unable to give much of a match even to the England XI of 1907, not an especially vintage year. They stood little chance, he thought, against that 1907 team – Fry, Hayward, Tyldesley, Foster, Hirst, Braund, Arnold, Douglas, Lilley, Rhodes and Buckenham. It was a good team. It shows the strength in depth of English cricket in 1907 even without some of the major names of the era, but I wonder if Sir Neville would still care to elevate it above that of 1930. He names them himself – Hobbs, Sutcliffe, Hammond, Hendren, Woolley, Jardine, Tate, Larwood, White, Robins and Duckworth!

In *The Times* of July 24, 1945, is a letter from James Agate, the famous drama critic and a close friend of Cardus. To the best of my knowledge, Sir Neville has never challenged its accuracy. Agate's memory of events following on Tom Richardson's herculean but vain bowling efforts at Old Trafford against Australia in 1896 was quite at variance with the following Cardus description.

> He stood at the bowling crease, dazed. *Could* the match have been lost? his spirit protested. Could it be that the gods had looked on and permitted so much painful striving to go by unrewarded? His body still shook from the violent motion. He stood there like some animal baffled at the uselessness of great strength and effort in this world. A companion led him to the pavilion, and there he fell wearily to a seat.

Agate gives in his letter firstly the memory of his friend H. J. Henley:

> ... after the winning hit Tom legged it to the pavilion like a stag and got down two pints before anyone else.

and secondly his own recollection:

> I can see the two Australians and eleven Englishmen legging it to the pavilion with the tall figure of Tom Richardson leading by many yards ...

and he concludes the letter by reminding us that he and Henley were present, Sir Neville was not:

> Cardus, who watched the great match at the age of seven from behind the bars of his nursery window some miles away, had the secret of higher truth. But on the lower ground he taradiddled.

The search for higher truth, and our receptivity to it is the stuff that powerful myths are made of. How much more satisfying a picture the dazed and stumbling Samson presents, than the ordinary man, a good day's work done, restoring his calories with a pint of bitter.

Another excellent example of time and distance lending enchantment, is the famous anecdote of Jessop's match at the Oval against Australia in 1902, when Hirst and Rhodes got the fifteen runs needed to win with Hirst scoring 13 singles in 14 strokes. On Rhodes' entry to the tension-packed arena, Hirst is supposed to have said to him 'We'll get them in singles, Wilfred'. As Rhodes made quite clear in a letter to Leslie Duckworth, the meticulous and entertaining biographer of Sydney Barnes, nothing of the sort transpired. As Rhodes put it;

> I don't remember Hirst saying anything to me when I joined him. That is all someone's imagination and the "We'll get them in singles" is ridiculous. After all if we could have got four fours it would have been just the same and over much quicker.

Those who would inject a little truth into this and similar legends are, in Cardus's words, 'solemn upholders of prosaic fact, people of that breed who are actually happy to kill a good story dead'. The answer to that is that fables spun with fictional characters are one thing, fables given us in the guise of historical fact are quite another.

Sir Neville has also written;

> When a man looks back over the years of acquaintance with the game, he does not see so many rounded events which happened in time and space. Rather does he feel flavours in the mind; history is transferred by recollection into essential characteristics and scenes, which together build up his idea of cricket. He forgets the transient particulars – he basks in an artist's sense of the eternal and representative values of universals.*

Unfortunately, the course of history is made up as much by 'transient particulars' as it is by the values of universals, and we neglect them at our peril. If we view Edwardian cricket only through partial eyes and memories, we will forget how successfully the propaganda papers over the petty snobbery, prejudices

*(Sir) Neville Cardus. *Cricket* (Longman).

and injustices which were just as much part of the scene as knife-edged flannels and flashing blades of willow.

No one minds a man extolling the virtues of Edwardian cricket and mourning its demise, providing that it is fully understood that those virtues were bought at a price, and that that price was the sacrifices of many for the glorification of the few. Charles Booth's *Life and Labour in London* of 1903 looked at the position of the professional. The wages were something in the range of 30s to 40s a week in the season, plus tips received for bowling at amateurs at practice nets. The MCC paid £4 for a win in a three day match at a representative match at Lord's and £3 10s for a loss. For an away game, the professional was given £5 to £6 for a three day match out of which he had to find his own fares and accommodation expenses. For a big match, e.g. Gentlemen v Players, the fee was £10 but that was naturally restricted to the few. Most players had to return to their trades in the winter although Surrey* (unlike the MCC) paid £1 a week or £1 10s to a few as a retaining wage. (By way of comparison, the earliest recorded payments in 1745 were one and a half guineas for an away match, and one guinea for a home match).**

Compared with the prevailing wages in industry, these figures are not bad, but as Booth says:

> Cricketers, especially first-class men, may be ranked among the lowest paid of all professional men. In power of drawing a paying crowd, a well-known eleven probably more than equals any music hall combination, and yet their remuneration will at best be but one quarter of that given to artistes.

Economics are one thing, status quite another. Sir Neville has rightly described George Gunn of Notts and England as 'an incalculable genius, a batsman of very rare personal skill, and of indefinite wit and caprice', but the 80 year old Gunn made it quite clear how much these sterling qualities had been appreciated at the game's headquarters:

> ... when I played, only amateurs were allowed in the Long Room. We professionals had to stay in our own quarters.

---

*Contrary to some accounts Yorkshire was not the first county to make all the year round payments – the honour belongs to Surrey.
**Rowland Bowen *Cricket: a history*, p. 51.

With separate entrances to the field on many grounds, and with separate changing rooms in others, there was much of the upstairs-downstairs aspect to cricket so far as amateurs and professionals were concerned. Sir Pelham Warner's 1903–4 England tour of Australia was the first time professionals were allowed to stay at the same hotel as the amateurs. The professionals, above all, were expected to know their (lowly) place. Sir Neville Cardus warmly commends George Hirst for a letter to Eton accepting the position of cricket coach:

> Not a word about 'terms', remuneration, salary, wages! Today the 'pro' would be pretty certain to make some stipulation regarding commission on sales of bats, balls, etc...

It was better if such men were kept in ignorance and given not what they might want, but what their betters thought was good for them. There was very little that could be called exploitation, but a very great deal of benevolent paternalism. C. L. R. James, the distinguished West Indian writer and one of the first to write on cricket 'beyond a boundary', when speaking of the solid Victorian class, which had appropriated cricket and made it their own national institution, put it like this: *

> Its chief subjective quality was a moral unctuousness. This it wore like an armour to justify its exploitation of common labour.

In the Edwardian era, there was less moral unctuousness, though much stress was still placed on the 'manliness' of the game, and certainly the embodiment of moral ethics implied in the phrases 'a straight bat' and 'it isn't cricket' held sway throughout the era and for long afterwards (perhaps as Mr James suggested, failing only to survive the bodyline controversy).

What I think characterises Edwardian cricket more truthfully than 'moral unctuousness', is the tendency to see a cricket ground as the last refuge from the urban sprawls that had resulted from the massive move of the population from the country into the towns. Only at such venues was it still possible to see vestiges of life as it had once been, or, rather, as people liked to think it had once been. It was a kind of artificial enjoyment by proxy of a long lost rural England populated by kindly

*C. L. R. James *Beyond a Boundary* 1963.

The French aristocrat
Baron Pierre De
Coubertin, father of the
modern Olympic
Games. Later he was a
man of peace but other
considerations interfered
in the 1890s

The stadium refurbished
for the 1896 Olympic
Games – note the
totally unsuitable track

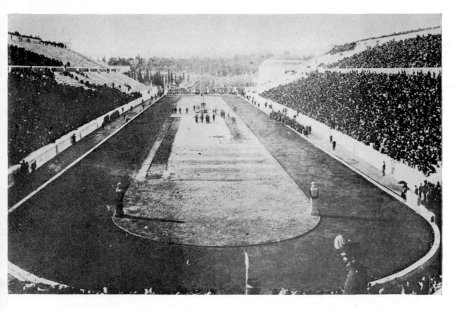

To the delight of the Greek crowd, Spyridon Loues wins the 1896 marathon for Greece

Left: Spyridon Loues in national costume leads the parade of winners at the 1896 Olympics. The Stars and Stripes and the elegantly dressed American college men show that the first modern Games was strictly for those who could afford to travel to Greece to compete. *Right:* The King of Greece, who did his best to enhance his own prestige at the 1896 Games, greets Loues who also reaped more tangible rewards from his win than a sprig of laurel

Dorando Pietri of Italy on his way from Windsor to the White City in the 1908 Olympic marathon. Refreshments from his two cycling attendants staved off exhaustion only temporarily

Dorando crosses the tape in the stadium but the illegal assistance from the Chief Clerk of the English officials on the left and Sir Arthur Conan Doyle on the right brought his disqualification after American protests

The 1908 marathon winner Hayes of America is hailed by his team-mates but the rest of the stadium remains indifferent

Queen Alexandra, to the evident satisfaction of De Coubertin (extreme right), presents her personal award, a special gold cup, to Dorando to console him for his disqualification

This picture of the five mile race in the 1908 Olympic Games shows the all too common empty terracing which was all London could muster for a world athletics festival

In sharp contrast to the White City, the 1908 Olympic rowing events at fashionable Henley drew large crowds, but English rowing was careful to prevent the ordinary man from competing

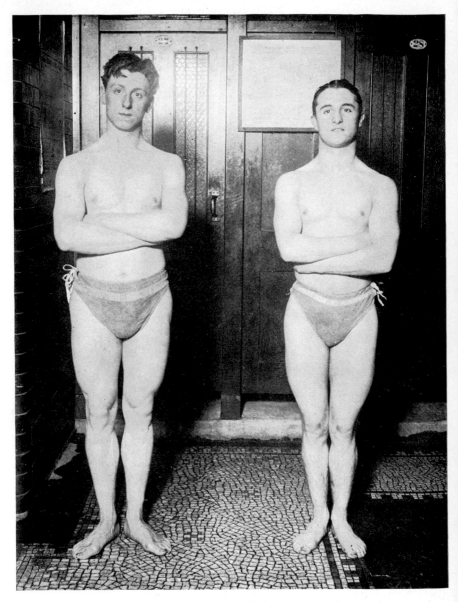

J. Sloane (left) and C. Stephens, two English swimmers photographed at an Olympic training session held at the Holborn baths before the 1912 Olympics. The casual nature of English preparations for Stockholm can perhaps be guessed from the fact the trunks are firmly labelled 'Borough of Holborn' and that Stephens has his on inside out

Jim Thorpe, the American half-Indian whose all round athletic ability won the 1912 Pentathlon and Decathlon on track and field, only for his awards and points to be stricken from the record books when it was disclosed that he had once played baseball for money

The 1913 Derby. Emily Davison, a suffragette lies dead on the turf after throwing herself under the King's horse – an Edwardian precedent for modern uses of sport for political ends?

squires and humble swains with rough exteriors but hearts of gold. That so cosy a picture owed more to a romantic kind of fiction, rather than to reality, did little to sap its tremendous power. And cast in the role of the honest yokel, uneducated but full of natural rustic humours, was the cricket professional. It seems no accident that such men were normally referred to as 'characters', for they were indeed expected to play a role in the play.

Sir Neville Cardus has done much to perpetuate the myth. Telling a story of an exchange passing between Emmott Robinson and Wilfred Rhodes, he concludes;

> These were 'county' characters, from mill and factory or pit, having horse sense and no more education than was needed in their condition of life. I have for years believed that a man should be thoroughly educated, or not at all.

If such men were given an education, they would no longer be prepared to play the roles already circumscribed for them, and worse, the advance of the common man would spoil things as they existed for the privileged and appreciative few. The Cardus attitude to this is also clear –

> I do not believe that anything fine in music *or in anything else* can be understood or truly felt by the crowd . . .
> (My italics)

Because the professional was a humbler being than the amateur, he was not to be exploited but to be treated with sympathy and understanding. He was not to be placed in a position where his lowly status might make him as vulnerable as a servant taking tea in the drawing room. Lord Hawke, captain of Yorkshire from 1883 to 1910 and later President of the MCC, wrote:

> There have always been disadvantages in having a professional as captain of a county team; for instance, he can be nagged at in the dressing-room by his fellows, and he is always liable to be a butt of grumblers, whilst he can never exercise the same authority as an amateur.

In a more private context, moving a vote of thanks at a Yorkshire AGM he was more virulent –

Please God, no professional shall ever captain England.

The Deity must have remained unimpressed, for in 1926 Jack Hobbs captained England in the Fourth Test against Australia at Manchester when amateur A. W. Carr was taken ill on the first day.

Another leading administrator, Lord Harris of Kent and England, shows that the position of the professional was not so much a matter of finance but of social standing:

> ... does he (the player) make his livelihood out of playing the game, is it his daily occupation in its season, does he engage himself day in and day out to play it from May 1 to August 31? If he does then he is a professional, *and he recognises as convenient and bows to those social regulations which distinguish the amateur and professional at cricket* ...* (My italics)

Lord Hawke's famous 'mark' system for the professionals in the Yorkshire team is an outstanding example of the paternalist approach. If a player made an outstanding catch or a notable innings, a mark went down in his lordship's pocket book. If he dropped a catch or got out foolishly, a blacker mark went down. At the end of the season, if the credits exceeded the debits, an envelope was handed to the player containing a sum of money calculated on the basis of the marks – a sort of accumulated tip for services rendered. In addition, players were not allowed access to any lump sums accruing at their benefits, that was safeguarded and administered by Hawke on their behalf, lest the windfalls led to short-sighted extravagance. He even looked out for the players' moral welfare – more than one touring party abroad found compulsory church attendance on Sundays an essential part of their duties.

That this kind of benevolent dictatorship was undertaken in well-meaning sincerity and from the best possible motives, is unquestionable, but how deeply illuminating of contemporary attitudes, and of the second-class citizenship of the professional.

There was never any question that cricket could be torn apart on the amateur/professional question in the ways that we have seen in rugby and soccer, for to all intents and purposes there

*In a letter to *The Times* in 1909.

had always been professionals in the game. The famous All England XI, started in 1846, the team of Clarke, Parr, Daft, Fuller Pilch, Mynn, Felix, and Wisden, was a team primarily of professionals (though some amateurs like Mynn and Felix were included), and fees were paid (about £5 a match). They toured England for some thirty years as did the breakaway United England XI, and they were primarily profit-making organisations.

In the pre-Victorian era, from the 1770's to the 1830's, cricket was shaped by the working man on the one hand, and its aristocratic sponsors and supporters on the other. Representative as they were of England's two nations, one doubts that either, particularly on the cricket field, were particularly conscious that there was a division, or that any such division was 'a state of things which ought not to be' (in the phrase of C. L. R. James). The French writer Edgar Joubert has also suggested that cricket played a great democratic part in lessening social tensions, for in place of the rigidity of the continental social systems, the game provided a step-ladder between the upper middle-class and the aristocracy, between the sporting snob and the ambitious middle-class son.*

Then, it was a game still, a medium for betting, and for that matter, an opportunity for the unscrupulous to buy and sell matches – the Regency mania for gambling brought many such perversions in its wake. It was only a later combination of Victorian morality – betting at Lord's died out only in the 1880s – and the elevation of cricket to the game 'which enshrined the Arnoldian and bourgeois virtues of Victorian England',** which saw the Barbarian and the Philistine united in keeping the professional in the place they wanted to see him – on the bottom rung holding the ladder firm with one hand and tugging at his forelock with the other.

In the 1860's, a man to whom all possible honour must be given, stepped on to the cricketing stage, commandeered the spotlight of public attention, and by his own unaided efforts showed what technical developments were possible in the game by the application of scientific principles. With the physical presence of a Macready, with the stature of a Gladstone, and with the

---

*In a sports magazine of 1864, it was said 'Prince, peer, parson, peeler and peasant all participate in the game.'

**See pages 26–7.

originality of a Darwin, this most eminent of Victorians was only to relinquish the spotlight in his mid-fifties with 54,896 runs, 2,876 wickets and 871 catches credited to him in the record books. He was, of course, William Gilbert Grace.

Grace was an amateur, a country doctor who became a national figure and made, by his presence, cricket a national game. Cricket, which had become dominated by professional bowlers unleashing their venom on pitches we would think akin to ploughed fields, and the venerable doctor became synonymous in the public mind as he flayed the highest class of bowling to the four corners of every major cricket ground in England. He built an immense following and in the process created modern batting. As Ranjitsinhji put it in *The Jubilee Book of Cricket*;

> He revolutionised batting. He turned it from an accomplishment to a science ... he turned its many narrow straight channels into one great winding river.

WG was imitated by every cricketer in the land – by the professional who had to encompass his discoveries or see a breadticket disappear, by the village cricketer who dreamed Walter Mitty-like of emulating the master, and by the public schoolboy for whom the game was assuming more and more importance. We will look at the public schoolboy more closely in a moment.

In the 1870's it was said that the Champion was past his best. It did not take him long to disprove it with innings after innings and one bowling performance after another. Some people never learned; they said it again in the 1880's and again he gave lie to the rumour. And by April 1895, the doubters were in a majority – the Old Man was 47, surely even he should call it a day. By the end of May, the Old Man had successfully fought off age and the credibility gap in a truly grand manner. His first innings of the season was for 103, a week later he scored 288, on May 23–5 he stayed on the field for an entire match against Kent helping himself to 257 and 73 not out, and finished the month with 1,016 runs under his belt. 1895 brought him by its close no less than 2,346 runs (the greatest aggregate of runs by anyone that season and including another 5 centuries). And he continued to open for England in his fifties.

In the Edwardian era, the apotheosis of a certain kind of cricket was reached – this was 'country-house' cricket. As much a part of the Edwardian country weekend as shooting and hunting parties for a houseful of guests, was the cricket match. Providing an opportunity for the talented amateur to spend half the summer travelling from one great country seat to another to be regally entertained and to play for the host's XI against one of the top wandering clubs like I Zingari or the Free Foresters, and played, even at the highest level in a not too competitive spirit, it was this kind of cricket which had two deprivations in succession finally to kill it off. Firstly the growth of the importance of county cricket made many first-class cricketers unavailable, and secondly, economic and social changes of the twentieth century brought the party to an end.

The complete antithesis of country-house cricket was league cricket. To the country-house set, the very concept of a league had all the connotations of the northern masses swaying, cheering and booing at football matches which were played not as elegant *entr'actes* between the lunch-time salad and the tea-time cucumber sandwiches, but first and foremost to win. It was not a concept which appealed to them.

In the same areas that league football had caught on, the 1890's saw the parallel spread of league cricket with clubs competing in the spirit of hard competitive rivalry. To its participants and its spectators, the idea that cricket was a game where gentlemanly conduct and cultivated display took precedence over the crucial item on the agenda of hammering the opponents into the ground, found neither makers nor takers.

These totally different conceptions of cricket can be seen as decisive influences in many a subsequent cricket argument – most of them too recent in the mind to need re-telling here (the chequered career of Brian Close to name but one example). And we are only seeing in cricket what we have already seen in football and rugby, so I need not dwell further.

The influence of the public school however, is so striking that we have to pay it more attention to understand the extraordinary flowering of batting talent in the Edwardian period. The public schoolboy found cricket fulfilling a major part of the school curriculum. Like the other sports, its supposed capacity to impart morality elevated it to an essential part of transforming him from a grubby anarchist to a fine Christian gentleman. Most public schools had a professional cricket coach and moreover a number of masters who were first-class amateurs in their own right and who were eager to pass on the rich heritage they had already themselves enjoyed. The boy's strokes were encouraged and corrected so that if he had any natural talent for the game it was likely to be fostered and brought to a kind of perfection before he went out into the university or the outside world.

For some mysterious reason, the strokes that were perfected and extolled tended to be on the offside of the wicket only. Although WG and his family would never have so limited themselves, and indeed did not, the public schoolboy was expected to play to the off like a gentleman and to eschew any pull to leg reminiscent of the village rustic. C. B. Fry, who later brought hard work, application and intellect to play in making himself an all-round batsman, was at Repton from 1888–91 and tells us that when he was there –

If one hit the ball in an unexpected direction to the on-side, intentionally or otherwise, one apologised to the bowler.

Alongside this sort of absurdity, very often went the idea that a success which had been worked for was of very little value compared with that due to natural talent. Ian Hay in *The Lighter Side of School Life* was, as the title suggests, being humorous but his words carry a factual basis:

What a boy admires most of all is ability – the ability to do things naturally and spontaneously . . . Great emphasis must be placed on the ease . . . you often hear such a conversation as this . . .

"Pretty useful, old Dobbin taking six wickets!"
"Oh, that rotter. Last year he could hardly get the ball within a yard of the crease. I hear he has been spending hours and hours in the holidays bowling by himself at a single stump. He's no earthly good, really."

It is the way of the world. The tortoise is a dreadfully unpopular winner. To an Englishman, a real hero is a man who wins a championship in the morning, despite the fact that he was dead drunk the night before.

It is also very striking that the amateur contribution to the game was so overwhelmingly one of fine batsmanship. Bowling, with its overtones of the professional slaving away in the nets dropping the ball on or about a length for the amateur to perfect his off-drive, was generally less attractive.* This can be over-stated, for quite a few amateurs became very good bowlers, but it has some general truth; in 1900 eighteen amateurs figured in the first twenty places in the season's batting averages, and in 1903, of the top twenty places in the bowling averages, a mere three went to amateur bowlers – facts at least indicative of a trend.

Confirmation of the generalisation can perhaps be seen too in the careers of two outstanding professional players – Robert Abel of Surrey, and Wilfred Rhodes of Yorkshire. Abel, one of the most consistent of batsmen when he was not troubled by recur-ring eyesight difficulties scored 32,669 runs in 994 innings for Surrey and England, including a 357 not out, yet his original engagement came as a bowler. Wilfred Rhodes, who formed so effective an opening partnership with Jack Hobbs by 1911–12 started his Test career in 1899 as a permanent number ten bats-man played for his bowling. Were it not for the unique qualities of the man, the late start might have given him more trouble in amassing the 39,802 runs he scored to add to his 4,187 wickets.**

Somehow the strength of the public school coaching which produced so many dazzling off-side strokes had to have a weak-ness built in to compensate. This weakness was a conservative reliance on the orthodox and on the done thing, sometimes to the detriment of common sense itself. Fry's story of the necessity to apologise for a hit on the leg side is a case in point. If we look at Ranji's famous *Jubilee Book of Cricket* of 1897, we find him, of all people, endorsing some very curious ideas on field-settings. Solemnly, he gives us, for example, the correct field for 'a medium right hand bowler on a good, fast/fast, wet/ or fiery wicket'. (!) He allows for two slips, short third man, point, cover, extra-cover, mid-off and on the on-side, a mid-on (long-on was optional and could be moved presumably into the gully, the slips, or perhaps extra extra-cover). In other words, one mid-on was found quite sufficient to cover the whole 180

*No bowler has ever received a knighthood for services to the game!
**The first of his 16 'doubles' came five seasons after his debut for Yorkshire.

degrees on the leg-side of the wicket. How could he do that? – because no well-brought up batsman was likely to play the ball there.

The supreme irony perhaps is that the striving for 'classical' stroke-play fostered in the schools, and imitated first by the amateur batsman, and later, for such things are infectious, by professional batsmen too (Jack Hobbs was frequently referred to as the professional who batted like an amateur), came to full fruition not with Englishmen at all but with an Indian and an Australian. This is not co-incidence, but an indication surely that batting genius gets to the top paying only lip-service to the orthodoxy of the day and owing very little to the coaching ideas that sustain the merely talented pupil. The careers of Trumper, of Ranjitsinjhi, of Bradman and of Compton are cases in point – they came to cricket as it was played, took what they wanted in the way of technique from imitation of their fellows, yet were prepared to defy the 'rules' and add individual idiosyncracies that a coach would have felt honour-bound to eliminate from their game.

Ranji, who came to Cambridge University from India, had little cricket background but a large private income, some of which he used to hire professional bowlers of the calibre of Tom Richardson and W. H. Lockwood of Surrey to bowl at him. In the face of the attack of two of England's finest bowlers, he taught himself two things – how to counteract his instinctive habit of pulling away from a fast ball, and how to overcome his diminutive stature by nimble enough footwork to get to the pitch of the ball and drive it, or to go on to the back foot and use the speed of the ball short of a length by helping it on its way to the boundary, with a delicate late cut or a fine leg glance. (Bradman, also short of stature, did much the same thing with cuts and pulls). Victor Trumper of Australia, came to England first with the 1899 Australians, though his sun shone brightest on the 1902 tour of England when he scored 2,570 runs and eleven centuries. Trumper too owed nothing to coaching and was prepared to use his magnificent eye to pull from the off-stump, cut off the middle or leg drive from outside the off regardless of the condition of the pitch. The individuality did not always bring consistency but hundreds of accounts confirm its unique excitement. Sir Neville Cardus has written

I have never met a cricketer who, having seen or played with Victor Trumper, did not describe him without doubt or hesitation the most accomplished of all batsmen of his acquaintance.

This is high praise, but it is not true. Rhodes thought there was no one to touch Bradman, and C. B. Fry wrote that Hammond had probably more charm and certainly took the laurel for pure mastery of technique. Rhodes and Fry both saw and played with Trumper.

The difficulty in trying to assess truly the merits of these batsmen of the 'golden age' is that even if their champions concede that modern field-placings and bowling tactics would have made the free-scoring of the times more difficult, there is always the fall-back to the infinitely subjective terminology of aesthetics – that the Trumpers and the Ranjis were superior to subsequent generations of players because of their 'style'. Sport, and other transient arts like acting, are always subject to such difficulties. In athletics, the cold hard facts of statistics show conclusively that the Ron Clarkes of today could give the Kolehmainens and the Nurmis laps and still beat them, but in cricket, although the figures are there by the thousands, so many variable factors like the quality of the bowling, the state of the wickets and so on, make comparisons relatively impossible.

Some things make me doubt that the 'style' was quite all it has been claimed subsequently. At the *Sunday Times* (1972) exhibition at the National Portrait Gallery, a rare snippet of news film was shown of Ranji and W. G. Grace in the nets. Tantalisingly brief, the strokes played by these two masters show the feet so far from the pitch of the ball as to make a modern bowler's mouth water. Also, a close examination of G. W. Beldam's book of photographs *Great Batsmen: their Methods at a Glance* often betrays the same tendency by many of the great batsmen to leave yawning gaps between bat and pad. (Apart from the famous picture of Trumper jumping out to drive, there is another tucked into the back of the book of the great Victor, being bowled neck and crop, with his head pointing somewhere towards the long-on boundary.) Many of the pictures are indeed models of technique and could serve in a contemporary textbook, but I think it significant that the faults are there although the technical demands of Edwardian photography meant that every picture had to be specially posed and the subjects were *not* necessarily doing what they would do in match conditions. (To emphasise this point it is only necessary to compare the posed photographs in, say, the average rugby textbook, with action pictures or slow-motion film taken during an international. Similarly, the great S. F. Barnes in full flight must have presented a very different picture to the posed photograph most commonly seen. Between what a man does in action and what he *thinks* he does in action can be two totally different things.)

Can we not also put down to the tempting gap between bat and pad, the success that Rhodes' partner in crime and punishment George Hirst reaped from 1902 onwards with the cricket ball? Up to 1901 he was a straightforward fast medium left arm bowler, but from that season he learnt in H. S. Altham's words, 'How to swing the ball, in and devastatingly late, and passed at once from the good to the great'. So great in fact that in the 1906 season, he scored a nice 2,385 runs, and once his pads were off, took 208 wickets (a double double likely to remain for ever in the record books as unique). He did the double in 17 separate seasons, and his career haul of 2,727 wickets cost him only 18.77 runs apiece.

By 1910, Lord Harris was complaining in *Wisden* that there was more bad batting than he could ever remember. He meant of course that there was less off-side play. He tells us that fielding had not altered except that three slips were now more common than two and a point, and that bowling was less accurate though there were more bowlers swerving the ball for a slip catch. He put the decline in style down to the tendency to get unnecessarily in front of the wicket, thereby cramping the batsman's room to make strokes.

Reading between the lines, does it not seem that a quite essential development had taken place? Faced with the problems of Hirst and his disciples bringing the ball in to the batsman late in flight, the batsman was forced to move across in front of the wicket to get behind the line and to eliminate the vulnerable 'gate' between bat and pad. This had become necessary for survival, for undoubtedly the batsman imbued with the desirability of making graceful strokes outside the off stump is doomed to failure unless the bowler obligingly keeps the ball there for him to do so.

Ranji's, Hirst's and Trumper's separate kinds of originality brought them rich awards at a time when orthodoxy was the norm and it is certainly originality which is the key to the career of B. J. T. Bosanquet, who, in Australia at least, is heralded by the use of the term 'bosie' for his invention of the googly. Bosanquet was a fine, forcing batsman with the added asset that he could always undertake a spell of orthodox medium pace bowling. At a session of 'twisty-grab', an inane game played with a tennis ball on a billiard table, he discovered that it was possible to turn the wrist as if for a leg-break but release the ball so that it spun on pitching from left to right or from off to leg. It became his party trick, and in the nets at Lord's he was occasionally persuaded to try it on batsmen with his friends rolling about in general hilarity. No one seemed aware that the sleight of hand might have general application to the game – it was not done because it was not one of the done things.

Perhaps for a dare, he tried it out in a match at Lord's in 1900 and the facing batsman, in all probability distracted by the general collapse of the Middlesex fielders, allowed himself to be bowled on the fourth bounce. But before the end of the season, he had the ball rather more under control, and a new style of bowling was born. Despite the fact that the invention was essentially a simple one, it was more than many could grasp. D. L. A. Jephson, in an article on leg-break bowling in the 1901 *Wisden* found it quite beyond comprehension:

> ... though his length is often eccentric he possesses the unique capability of delivering a ball with every semblance of a leg-break, which on striking the pitch turns inches from the off. Whether this can be done at will, or whether it is the gift of the blind goddess, I cannot tell ...

Bosanquet's brand of deceit was to achieve two great England victories over Australia. In the Fourth Test at Sydney in February 1904, Australia in their second innings, wanting 329 to win with the pitch getting easier and easier stood at 74 for 3 and when Bosanquet came on collapsed in disorder to 171 all out. Bosanquet took 6 for 51 but the deed was mightier than the figures. He wreaked similar havoc in 1905 at Trent Bridge. In the

Australian second innings, Duff and Darling were playing out confidently for a draw as Bosanquet struggled to find a length, then it all came right for him, the Australians became mesmerised and returned swiftly to the pavilion leaving Bosanquet with the memorable figures of 8 for 107. Australia 188 all out.

Instead, however, of the invention and its creator founding a school of English googly bowlers, the idea was taken up elsewhere in the world – by the South Africans. Bosanquet's disciples were Schwarz, Vogler, Faulkner and White. Bosanquet taught Schwarz the technique and he taught others so that the 1907 South Africans in England commanded no less than four leg-break bowlers in their attack. There were individual differences – Schwarz himself bowled only off-breaks with the leg-break action but they came slow through the air, then nipped off the pitch, turning up to a yard on a sticky wicket, and he bowled to six men on the on-side of the wicket; Vogler was faster through the air, had only three men on the off-side, and concentrated on leg-breaks with a disguised googly about once in two overs and an even deadlier top-spinner that won him many an l.b.w. decision; Faulkner and White were much of a muchness, fast off the pitch and with the occasional 'wrong-un'.

The quartet showed how the original idea could be developed. Rather late in the day, the 1908 *Wisden* thought '...this new kind of bowling is a very great invention'. (South Africa failed to win a test but the atrocious weather was usually against them, so were the umpires, said some, and their batsmen never really solved the problems presented by Colin Blythe on a rain-affected wicket). The curious thing is that it took the Springboks to show what could be done with the 'very great invention'.

One hazards the reason that again Edwardian orthodoxy had triumphed over original enterprise. So concerned were they and their later champions to present a united front to the world, that facts which did not comfortably fit in with the cosy chosen image tended to be ignored (and in this, how naturally Edwardian Sir Neville Cardus appears). It is only when one examines the calm pond-like surface of Edwardian cricket closely and critically that one becomes aware of the bubbles of dissent that sometimes broke the surface.

In August 1896 the inferior status and treatment of the professional and his genuine grievances led to a strike in the selected

Test match team for the Oval. There was still no central selection and each ground authority selected the England team when they were host to a test. The Surrey committee announced nine certainties to play and four names from which the last two places would be chosen. When the team was given out, a letter was received by the Surrey committee from Lohmann, Abel, Gunn, Richardson and Hayward who refused to play unless the fee went up from £10 to £20. There was general consternation, particularly as four of the militants were Surrey players – they were accused of stabbing their employers in the back, elevating money-grubbing above the honour of representing their country and so on.

The pressure brought to bear was too much and just like the later players' strike in soccer, the ranks divided and fell. Two days before the match, Abel, Hayward and Richardson withdrew from their stand and a meeting on the morning of the match agreed to let them play after all. Gunn, supported by Lohmann, stood out for the principle although Lohmann later gave in and apologised to the committee. The match took place without them.

Even though the strike collapsed so suddenly, rumours concerning excessive expenses being paid to amateurs continued and C. W. Alcock (secretary of Surrey in addition to his role at the Football Association) took space in the 1897 *Wisden* for a statement denying authoritatively that W. G. Grace had been paid any more than £10 to cover his expenses for the Oval Test. It was a powerful answer to the rumours but it neglected to mention two things – that WG over the season got £2,377 2s 6d in a testimonial so he hardly needed more than £10; and that the Surrey committee had paid out £20 to Alfred Shaw, Morley and Barnes for a test appearance under Lord Harris against Australia a decade before. *Wisden* was relatively coy about shamateurism generally and added

> Mr W. G. Grace's position has for years, as everyone knows, been an anomalous one, but 'nice customs curtsey to great kings' and the work he has done in popularising cricket outweighs a hundredfold every other consideration.

Indeed it did and all honour to the Doctor. But that is no counter to the powerful case of the English professionals that whereas they were expected to play for a £10 fee, their Australian opponents, who were all amateurs, would be sharing out the proceeds of the tour and going home with a very tidy sum indeed.

If they toured Australia themselves a very different arrangement held sway, particularly if we are to believe the E. A. Murrow cartoon of 1911, which C. B. Fry, surely a man to judge its accuracy, thought worthy of including in his magazine. In the drawing John Bull speaks to a white-flanelled cricketer:

'Yes my dear fellow, I expect you to go to Australia for half a year to uphold my prestige in cricket. It will cost you £250. I will allow you £70 ... You lose half a year's income too ... I fear I cannot help that, you must stand the loss. The Australian clubs and the MCC will no doubt make several thousands profit ... there it is!

Other ripples which crossed the glass-like surface of the cricket millpond came from a most surprising quarter, the Oxford v Cambridge match at Lord's. The 1893 Varsity match was a great draw – 18,000 people saw the first day, and just under 20,000 the second day. Cambridge batted first and scored 182 in their first innings. Oxford in reply were 95 for 9 as the last man came to the wicket. Now the follow-on rule as it stood at the time was that an 80 run deficit on the first innings meant a follow-on, a *compulsory* follow-on at that. Three more runs were scored, leaving Oxford still 84 behind and with 5 runs needed to save the follow-on. The pitch was easy enough and it was to Oxford's advantage to throw the last wicket away and bat again. A mid-pitch conference between the batsmen reached the obvious conclusion, but before they could sacrifice the last wicket, they had been either out-thought or overheard by the Cambridge captain (F. S. Jackson). Wells the bowler bowled the first ball of the next over wide to the boundary (102 for 9), failed to get the next wide enough although it was bowled all along the floor, but put the total to 106–9 with the third – a round-arm sling to the boundary. The follow-on had been averted.

Great was the discussion after the match of the ethics involved in this wholly defensible piece of gamesmanship with A. E. Stoddart and W. G. Grace declining an invitation to comment in the next issue of *Wisden*. But where the mighty feared to tread, others rushed in and out of the commotion came a new ruling that the follow-on would still be compulsory but would be lifted to a 120 run deficit (A good example of an MCC compromise getting the worst of both worlds).

The inevitable happened, and it happened moreover again at the University match, this time in 1896. Oxford had the satisfaction of winning the match by four wickets. Cambridge had the disappointment of losing but also a barrage of criticism to face for a repetition of the tactics of 1893. Cambridge batted most of the first day for 319. Oxford got within 131 runs of them but lost nine wickets in doing so. Frank Mitchell, the Cambridge captain, perhaps remembering the precedent set by F. S. Jackson, decided he would far rather bat again than field. Under orders, Shine the bowler at the Nursery End bowled the next three balls, two of them no-balls, direct to the boundary for 12 extras and the follow-on was averted.

So deeply did Mitchell's tactic offend those who saw cricket as something on a higher spiritual plane than just a game, the Cambridge team were booed, jeered and actually jostled and manhandled by MCC members inside the pavilion.* And the whole affair sparked a long correspondence in *The Times* which divided even brother against brother (Lord Cobham and Edward Lyttleton). Unless this incident can be seen in terms of a society trying desperately to uphold an artificial moral code and deeply suspicious of and hostile to any action which threatened the *status quo* – the normal attitude of die-hards – its attendant virulence would be inexplicable.**

With the professionals' strike and the Varsity match, 1896 was not much of a vintage year for cricket but there was another wholly discreditable episode in the season that cannot be forgotten. Harry Trott's Australians, whose fluctuating fortunes made this a tour to remember were a strong all-round side. They had Gregory, Darling, Iredale, Giffen, Trott and Clem

*This unseemly commotion was nearly repeated in the First Test of the 1905 series against Australia at Nottingham. Shouts, boos, jeers and general displeasure were directed at bowler Armstrong and captain Darling for trying to mitigate a commanding England lead and the paucity of the Australian attack by bowling consistently wide of the leg stump.

**Only after a deal of heat had been engendered was the limit of the follow-on raised to 150 runs (it is now 200) in 1900 and the essential abolition of the compulsory clause carried out.

Hill* to get runs and in attack they could call on Jones for pace, McKibbin to turn the ball and Trumble who could turn the ball at medium pace and was a master at setting his own fields. In the MCC match at Lord's eleven days before the First Test, they were caught on a dreadful wicket. Their innings standing at the worrying total of 18 for 3, Pougher came on to bowl. At his hands, the rapid demise of the innings was not long delayed. From 18 for 3, the Australians were 18 all out and Pougher finished with an analysis which receives scarce attention in many record books of 3–3–0–5 (!) At the other end Hearne took 4 for 4 as a prelude to taking 9 for 73 in the Australian second innings.

The defeat was not looked on as in any way representative of Australian form, and the England XI announced in the following week was eagerly scrutinised for potential weaknesses in case the Australians should revenge the defeat they had sustained at home from A. E. Stoddart's party in the winter of 1894–5. There was one glaring omission – K. S. Ranjitsinhji, at the height of his powers and on his way to 2,780 runs for the season. Glosses with regard to his qualification for England have been placed on this omission, but the hard fact is that he was left out because of the virulence of colour prejudice at Lord's (remember the ground authorities were responsible for selection of the team).

Similar prejudice had reared its ugly head at Cambridge where Ranji's Blue was in some danger of never coming – he got it in his third year – for similar reasons. We have the word of Sir Home Gordon that

> ... there was so much prejudice against "a nigger showing us how to play cricket"...

and so common was this view that Sir Home was threatened by a veteran player, who had both played for the Gentlemen

---

*To show that despite its hold on the national consciousness, not every Englishman falls under the spell of cricket, I cannot resist adding here an anecdote told of Sir Malcolm Sargent. On a visit to Australia, a host, with the traditional Australian hospitality, asked him if he would like to go to see Clem Hill. Ever the perfect guest, Sir Malcolm replied "Certainly I would – how high is it?"

and served on the MCC committee, with expulsion from the MCC if he had

... 'the disgusting degeneracy to praise a dirty black'...

Sir Home also put Ranji's habit of wearing his sleeves buttoned at the wrists down to a sensitive desire 'to mitigate his dusky appearance'.

It is encouraging to record that at least the Old Trafford and the Oval authorities snubbed the MCC heavily by inviting Ranji to join the England team for the other two tests: invitations to which he responded by crucifying the Australian bowling at Manchester with 62 and 154 not out (in 190 minutes and hitting 23 fours), and running out Iredale at the Oval with a whirlwind throw from over 100 yards away from the wicket.

The treatment of Ranji was not the only example of colour prejudice to grace the golden age. The political roots of South African apartheid stemming partly from the Boer War settlement also lie within its years, with the result that the 1894 tour of England by a South African party was undertaken without an outstanding fast bowler, T. Hendricks, purely because he was of Far Eastern extraction. And although the 1910–11 South African party to Australia included a coloured all-rounder in C. B. Llewellyn, who had played for Hampshire, he was subjected to a number of unpleasant indignities at the hands of his fellow white tourists, to the extent to having to lock himself in hotel lavatories to escape them.*

In the number of moral, political, racial and class prejudices which have their roots in Edwardian period, it is possible to see problems which have continued to plague the sport. To take just one, the apartheid issue which raised its head then and was ignored, returned in greater force at the end of the 1920's when Duleepsinhji was dropped from the England team to mollify the feelings of the touring South Africans and discreetly not picked when reciprocal tours were made. In its turn this led to the whole sorry charade of the sixties when the totally untenable South African attitude to Basil D'Oliveira still found the MCC (as indeed it did the Rugby Football Union on a similar issue) glaringly insensitive to the moral implications of continuing to play against South Africa, and trying desperately to paper over

Cricket: a history, p. 150.

the cracks with the comforting cliché that politics should not be allowed to interfere with sport thus blithely ignoring the fact that the politics had been placed firmly in the sport by the South Africans seventy years before.

A rather more healthy bequest that comes down to us from the years before the First World War, though sadly increasingly an anachronism, is the County Championship. Lord Harris tells us that he was originally laughed at at an MCC dinner for urging young gentlemen amateurs to give up their country-house cricket to support their county. His gospel soon found less stony ground and the nineties saw significant developments. In 1890 a mere eight counties competed, but in 1891 Somerset joined; in 1895 so did Derbyshire, Essex, Hampshire, Leicestershire and Warwickshire; and late stragglers Worcestershire in 1899 and Northants in 1905 completed the picture.*

A short lived County Cricket Council constituted by Lord Harris in 1887 went the way of all flesh in December 1890, but the official County Championship (an unofficial one had flourished for over twenty years) began in 1890 and from 1894 the MCC had a hand in controlling it. Methods of deciding how the Championship should be won have been more numerous than the counties competing, but just in our period, the methods were these:

1890–94	Losses deducted from wins and draws ignored.
1895–1909	1 point for a win, 1 point deducted for a loss, drawn games ignored. The champions to be those with the greatest number of points proportionate to the number of possible points in the finished games actually decided.
1910	Percentage of matches won to matches played.
1911–1914	5 points for a win, 3 points for 1st inns lead, 1 point losing on 1st inns. Placings to be decided by percentage of points won to possible points in the matches played.

As can be seen, the formula took some deciding (it has ever since too) and some odd anomalies cropped up under the different systems. The new system of 1895 in the event meant that that season the places from 8th to 14th were counted in minus points.

*Glamorgan only achieved first class status in 1921.

In 1896, Yorkshire the champions played 26 fixtures, Essex down the table played only 12. In 1897, Lancashire (P–26 W–16 L–3 D–7) had 13 points. So did Surrey (P–26 W–17 L–4 D–5) but Surrey finished second when all the calculations had been done. The short lived system of 1910 was an idea stemming from Lancashire. Kent became champions with 76.00%. Surrey were second with 57.14% which was a pity for Lancashire because they finished fourth and would have finished second if they had stuck with the old system!

It was within the framework of county cricket, despite its problematical mathematics, that a whole class of amateur batsmen emerged to grace the game with 'style', and the counties and the England XI in turn were privileged to see some remarkable men and some equally remarkable innings. The class of player whom Lord Harris had urged to leave the country-house set and join his county displayed his talents before large crowds of cricket spectators who had never seen a country-house in their lives. Their names and their deeds loom large in the annals of the game.

There was the patrician and autocratic Maclaren; the mighty Jessop, always liable to set loose a spell of ferocious hitting to make the fastest of attacks look as innocuous as underhand lobs; F. S. Jackson, who trounced the 1905 Australians almost single-handed, winning the toss five times and heading both the batting and bowling averages; the elegant and coolly poised R. H. Spooner; Lionel Palairet, another stylist whose Test career was restricted to just four innings by the all round strength of English batting in his day; the neat and efficient Pelham Warner; the speedy and delicate R. E. Foster and many others like the now forgotten Major R. M. Poore, a 6 ft 4 in man who used his height and strength to drive the ball ferociously and was the sensation of the 1899 season when he played a mere 16 innings for 1,399 runs and an *average* of 116.58. Their careers and their styles have been recorded by far more skilful pens than mine and their claim to fame is assured, but I think it is often forgotten that the truism, that it is bowlers who win matches, applied just as much then as since.

No bowler can work miracles, and a good total to bowl against and a skilful captain to place fields and vary the attack are un-questionably necessary to win anything, but the three counties

143

who dominated the Championship from 1890 to 1914 did so because of the strength of professional bowling that they could command. Of the 25 final tables, these three, Surrey, Yorkshire and Kent between them topped 20 of them. From 1890 to 1899 Surrey won the Championship more often than not and they did so by producing three fine fast bowlers in George Lohmann, Tom Richardson and Bill Lockwood. From 1900 to 1908 they were succeeded by Yorkshire, their main rivals of the Nineties. That Yorkshire could bowl Rhodes, Hirst and Schofield Haigh (Haigh in 1905 and 1906 took 342 wickets at under 14 runs each, did five hat-tricks and took 8 wickets in an innings on seven occasions*) had much to do with the Tykes' supremacy. Kent's first win came in 1906 and they followed it with three more in 1909, 1910 and 1913 – the feats a direct result of the foundation of a Tonbridge nursery in 1897 which put a pool of professional talent at their disposal. And a team which could command the deadly slow left arm of Colin Blythe, the speed of Fielder (25 wickets in a series in Australia), and the all-round assets of Frank Woolley, could certainly be expected to win things.**

The 1914 *Wisden* was relatively ungracious about Kent's 1913 win though conceding the reason – 'It was regrettable ... to find Kent so largely dependent on professional talent'. What *Wisden* had not grasped was that cricket had developed in parallel with soccer and that the ultimate successes were going to be claimed by those who brought not only talent to the game but full-blooded dedication and application too. The great days of the amateur, who, in Ian Hay's light hearted phrase, could 'win a championship in the morning, despite the fact that he was dead drunk the night before' were not ended by the First World War, in cricket and football they were already over before it broke out.

Because the trend is unpalatable to many, there is often a reluctance to recognise the phenomenon. Surely much of the criticism levelled in our own time at Geoffrey Boycott has its

---

*Of his 1,940 career wickets, no less than 1,138 were clean bowled!

**Nottinghamshire's solitary win in 1907 reinforces the point even more strongly – none of their batsmen reached an average of 33 and two bowlers carried the attack almost single handed. The bowling figures were A. W. Hallam: Overs 804, Maidens 259, Runs 1803, wickets 153, Average 11·78. T. Wass: Overs 761·1, Maidens 188, Runs 1969, Wickets 145, Average 13·07. All other bowlers only mustered 450·4 overs between them.

foundations in an unwillingness to see Boycott's career for what it is – the colossal achievement of a man, without a host of god-given talents, who by his own efforts has made himself into a great cricketer. Recognising that he would never be capable of an innings like that of Dexter in the Lord's Test against the West Indies in 1963 (surely a spectacular throw-back to the days of Jessop), and, like Barrington before him, he has understood the implications, and bought success by paying the price of dedication and eschewing anything that smacks of holding a hostage to fortune. What is unfair is to blame him personally because he happens to be the living embodiment of the changes in the game that economic and social factors have wrought. Naturally total admiration is reserved for the man who can come to a system and by his natural genius impose his will upon it; but is there no honour for the Boycotts who take a system and its implications and operate so brilliantly within it? It would be sad if we found no place in our hearts for the latter as well as the former.

If we seek a continuity in the development of modern batsmanship from W. G. Grace its founder, to the present day, the inescapable conclusion is that the Spooners and the Palairets now look to be the brief flowering of a minor school doomed to leave little but warm memories for the use of the future. Products of a particular social environment, they reflected something of the grace and elegance of that age, but by the nature of things could do little to influence subsequent developments. We can honour them and their achievements as we do Whistler and Sargent in painting but seventy years on we need also to look for the equivalent of Cezanne. I would suggest that two men played a vital role in laying the foundations for men of later generations to follow – one an amateur and one a professional.

The first is C. B. Fry. Perhaps the most gifted natural athlete of his day – he played rugby at a high standard, held the world long jump record for twenty-one years, played soccer for England and appeared in an F.A. Cup Final with Southampton – he brought to cricket his fine physical attributes, but, more importantly, he brought a razor sharp intellect to bear on the game (he was something of a Renaissance man for he was also a noted classical scholar) and in particular on the art of batsmanship. Originally he bowled as well but his action, considerably less classical than his reading, was frowned on by authority, and after being no-balled for throwing by Umpire Phillips (the Sid Buller of his day) he concentrated on his batting. (Phillips' attempts to uphold the rule of law clearly rankled for Fry wrote forty years later that Phillips was 'ambitious to achieve the reputation of a "strong umpire" '.*)

Unbounded by the tradition of his school for off-side play, he analysed batting as it existed and found scientific answers to any delivery which would be likely to dismiss him. As a result, he cut across contemporary opinion and became notable for adding impregnable backplay to his well timed drives, and for scoring the majority of his runs on the on-side of the wicket. Consequently, though Ranji monopolised the eye at Sussex matches, it was Fry at the other end who consistently piled up good scores. In 658 innings he amassed over 30,000 runs for an *average* of over 50, he topped the English batting averages in six different seasons (averaging over 70 in four of them), he fell only six short of a hundred centuries, in 1901 alone he scored over 3,000 runs, and in 1903 his successive scores from the end of June to September read 74, 28, 200, 5, 232 n.o., 160, 22 n.o., 99, 127 n.o., 98, then 4 and 0 (both to George Hirst in a match against Yorkshire) and to show the two low scores were a temporary aberration, 138 and 101 n.o. against Kent. H. S. Altham has said of Fry, 'his batting never revealed itself as an art.' If that is so, as a testament to craftsmanship his figures speak for themselves.

In the First Test at Edgbaston against Australia in 1909, a rain affected wicket produced all sorts of fun and games. An Australian team that included Bardsley, Armstrong, Trumper, Noble, Gregory and Macartney was skittled out by Hirst and Blyth for a mere 74 runs, a total that looked healthier after the England first innings produced only 121. Australia, again stumbling to Hirst and Blythe, got another 151 runs which left

*For a man so splendidly free of cricketing prejudices, Fry had a host of social and political ones. He backed Lord Roberts' campaign to make 'Britain ready to resist invasion by foreign powers' with his own campaign to get rifle clubs started throughout the country; he was still expressing admiration for Hitler and for Hitler's methods in 1939. The formal discipline of Hitler's Youth compared with the Boy Scouts was 'a distinct point of superiority on the German side' and so far as Nazi Germany was concerned, 'the atmosphere of effective discipline strangely appealed to me . . . everybody knew his allotted place and went there when called'.

England 105 to win, a meagre enough total on paper but bound to present fearsome difficulties on a worn and turning wicket. Fry, who had been dismissed first ball in the first innings, opened the English batting with a young man playing in his first test in England* and who, like Fry, was on a king-sized 'pair'. Fry's youthful partner was John Berry Hobbs, destined to be arguably the best batsman England has ever produced.

On that treacherous wicket, Fry scored 35 not out but even he had to concede supremacy to the newcomer who scored 62 not out, a piece of defiant batsmanship worth 200 in more normal circumstances, as the two of them stayed together to win the match by ten wickets. Jack Hobbs' innings that day, said Fry thirty years later, was 'as great an innings as I ever saw played by any batsman in any Test match or in any other match'. And as the verdict delivered by the one eye-witness better placed to observe it than anyone else, who are we to question it?

As Jack Hobbs had begun, so he duly continued. Taking up the baton handed on to him by Grace and Fry, he carried it nobly and worthily through the rest of the Edwardian era, through the Twenties and up to the Thirties to relinquish it only to Wally Hammond. He took mastery of back-foot play from Fry, he took beauty and variety of stroke from his other Edwardian contemporaries, and he married them together in a way as to justify the tag 'the Master'. Even if every photograph and piece of film of his play were to be destroyed, his figures alone would leave ample evidence that here was a great batsman. 61,237 runs in his career for an average of 50.65; 5,410 runs in tests against the best bowling of two separate generations; 197 centuries; twenty-six times over 1,000 runs for a season; such statistics speak for themselves. And can there be a more powerful pointer that his successes stemmed not from the transient speed of hand and eye of youth, but from a mastery of batting technique, than the fact that of his 197 centuries no fewer of 98 of them were made *after* he had passed the age of forty. Against increasing developments of spin and seam bowling from the resumption of cricket in 1919 onwards, Hobbs was an Edwardian who not only survived but dominated. In opening partnerships it was Hayward and Hobbs, then Rhodes and Hobbs, then Sandham and Hobbs, then Sutcliffe and Hobbs, but whether the partner-

*He had already represented England in Australia.

ship was for Surrey or for England, it was Hobbs who was ever-present. He shared in first wicket stands of over 100 no less than 166 times, and 28 of them lasted at least another hundred runs as well. He and Rhodes put on 323 for the first wicket against Australia at Melbourne in 1911–12, and 221 against South Africa at Cape Town in 1909–10; he and Sutcliffe put on 283 against Australia at Melbourne in 1924–5, and 268 against South Africa at Lord's in 1924 – in the history of cricket there must have been a few backs a fielding side would rather see than Hobbs's returning to the pavilion.

One would love to have the space to include in this chapter descriptions of all the tours to and from Australia made from 1890 to 1914, but so many detailed re-creations have been written already that they would be superfluous to a general account. Suffice it to say that although tours to and from the West Indies, South Africa and America took place, it was unquestionably the fifteen series against Australia that commanded the lion's share of attention. For the record, of the 63 matches played in the period, England won 23 and Australia 25, the other 15 were drawn (not exactly overwhelming statistical evidence of a golden age of English cricket).

An interesting experiment that took place in the 1912 season of a Triangular Tournament between Australia, England and South Africa but held in England foundered for a number of reasons. The weather made the season one of the wettest ever, the South African standard was not high although two South African bowlers, Pegler and Faulkner returned home with 189 and 163 tour wickets respectively, and the Edwardian public showed conclusively that international sport was only attractive providing England were involved – the two Tests between Australia and South Africa deliberately held at the Whitsun and August Bank Holiday weekends to attract crowds were very poorly supported. (The few who went to Manchester to see the first of the two, got something pretty unique for their money – T. J. Matthews of Australia taking a hat-trick in each South African innings). As we shall see, narrow patriotism was an omnipresent too in another kind of international sport – the Olympic Games.

CHAPTER FIVE

He Who Cannot Make Sport
Should Mar None

(Old Scottish proverb)

In an examination of one of sport's most extraordinary phenomena, we can do no better than to look first at the Concise Oxford Dictionary for a definition of the word 'Olympian'.

Olŷm'pian, a, & n. 1. Of Olympus, celestial; (of manners etc.) magnificent, condescending, superior; = foll. 2. n. Dweller in Olympus, one of the greater ancient-Greek gods; person of super-human calmness and detachment.

The definition betrays one of the most striking factors in the foundation of the modern Olympic movement in the 1890's – that it was very far removed from what we like ideally to call a quadrennial opportunity for men and women to compete against their fellows regardless of their race, religion and class. It was, on the contrary, deliberately exclusive and anti-democratic. Instead of being a sports event held for open competition, it was from the very outset a spectacular attempt by a minority of Barbarian and Philistine Edwardians to organise a massive and segregated international garden party held behind tall impenetrable hedges designed to keep the proletarian masses on the outside.

When the father of the Modern Olympics died in the late 1930's he was lauded with international honours as an idealist and a man of peace. Baron De Coubertin of France, for such was he, deserved most of the praise which was laid at his feet, for after the First World War when European statesmen generally ranged from unscrupulous power maniacs to helpless blunderers teetering into the horrifying pit of a Second World War, his was one of the few voices raised for sanity and reason. This was

149

not however the same De Coubertin who fathered the Olympic movement.

To understand the motives of the young French aristocrat without whom the modern Olympic movement might never have emerged from the womb, or alternatively been as disastrously still-born as the ill-fated League of Nations, we have to return to France of the 1870's. Helpless in the face of Teutonic military efficiency, De Coubertin's countrymen had just lost the Franco-Prussian War disastrously. Gloriously yet stupidly, the dashing élan of the beloved French cavalry charge had been blown to the four winds by the fire and destruction belching from the mouths of German cannons, as doomed and as fatally attracted as a moth beating its wings at a candle flame. The French, a conquered people, brought to their knees, some of their most sacred tenets strewn across their own battlefields, needed above all else someone to restore their shattered morale and to show them the way back to their traditional status as a major European power.

This was a greater task than any one man could accomplish, let alone a youth who only reached his majority in 1884, but within these limitations, De Coubertin did his best. Not that he went out into the streets to drum up support, but he used his considerable wealth to travel widely and to entertain on a vast scale – he was after not the support of the people but the friendship of the leaders of society, the opinion makers and ultimately the policy makers.

With a heavyweight statesman in Bismarck, and undergoing an industrial revolution which took the virtues of the British one without the mistakes inevitable on being first in the field, Germany from the 1870's was growing economically, militarily and politically to European supremacy. Much of her success was built upon an educational system, and along with the system went the German fascination for aristocratic Hellenic ideals and the doctrines of 'super-man' embedded in the work of the then contemporary Nietzsche.

De Coubertin saw the German successes, he saw the underlying philosophies and he drew conclusions. However, to propogate German ideas and advocate German remedies to French problems stood no chance of success with leaders of a society which had been on the receiving end of German success in the least welcome way. De Coubertin saw the defeat of 1870 as 'conclusive evidence of the deterioration of the quality of the French people from some earlier zenith of moral, and, most particularly, physical perfection' (a quotation for which I am indebted to Richard Mandell's *The Nazi Olympics* and in which a more comprehensive account of these factors than I can give will be found). Instead of looking to Germany, De Coubertin looked to England to take advantage of the French aristocrat's fondness for things English.

Here was another great European power, perhaps there was something in the English educational system which could explain English international supremacy. He paid his first visit to England in 1884, and many thereafter, he toured English public schools and he liked what he saw. There was the look to Greece and Rome in the classical curriculum, and there were moreover elements of moral discipline, manliness and strength clearly resulting from the English fondness for games. Games, as the foreword to his book *The Evolution of France* put it, were 'the best sort of protection to the young men of our times from the temptation to unworthy indulgences that tend to undermine personal vigor and thereby to diminish the vitality of the nation'.

On his return to France, he began to preach the gospel of athletics as an essential to the French school curriculum, but *not* just because he liked sport:

It was, therefore, with no mere boyish fondness for the excitement of athletic contest, considered as a thing desirable in itself, that M. de Coubertin devoted himself to the development or the revival of a high type of manhood among French students.

He wrote articles, he published a book on English education, he visited America to look at college sport, and his reputation and his doctrine grew to the extent that at the Paris Exposition of 1889 he was asked to launch a Committee for the Propagation of Sports and Physical Exercises in Education, and in 1891 he organised the Union des Societes des Sports Athletiques. The new Union canvassed for English and American competitors to visit France to keep the interest in sport going.

The following year, 1892, at a lecture at the Sorbonne, he revealed his thoughts that there should be a revival of the ancient

Olympic Games. The applause was less than deafening and though he took the idea to America and to Britain, it was hardly a surefire winner. Instead of abandoning the product, he repackaged it in a new wrapping and marketed it more carefully.

De Coubertin called a congress to be held in Paris for June 1894 to discuss that increasingly painful problem for sports administrations – how to define the amateur in terms which would both successfully exclude the growing numbers of participants who were of too lowly an economic status to play without pay and preserve the spiritual ethic embedded in the amateur ideals of manliness induced by participation in sport. Delegates arrived for the conference and spent a few pleasant days discussing the amateur problem, yet most of their time was spent at De Coubertin's lavish luncheons and banquets where they were wined and dined and lulled into a receptive frame of mind. At the end of the conference, to the accompaniment of a choir singing a spurious 'Hymn to Apollo' the announcement was made of a new Olympics, a modern edifice to realise the Hellenistic aristocratic ideals of Ancient Greece, and one to be held in Paris in 1900 as part of the International Exhibition when it was hoped the world and his wife would be in Paris.

Carried away with the idea and with the references to Ancient Greece, the Greek delegate came up with a further refinement. As the ancient Olympics were held every four years, why not start, not in Paris in 1900 by which time enthusiasm might have dissipated, but in Athens, the home of the ideal? A Games in Athens in 1896 would get the thing off to a fitting start for 1900. This was even more favourably received and the delegates went home with a warm rosy glow, knowing that they had struck a blow for authoritarian and reactionary ideas on sport. De Coubertin's favoured friends among them were formed into an International Olympic Committee.

When the Greek delegate got home he was confronted with much enthusiasm for the idea but little practical assistance from a bankrupt government. The indefatigable De Coubertin went hot-foot to Greece and helped to rescue the situation by some more wining and dining of people likely to contribute funds. Somehow enough cash was accumulated for a totally unsuitable stadium of white marble to be furbished for the occasion; the Stamford Bridge groundsman was imported to lay a cinder track of loose and impeding cinders; a British athletics coach was imported to drill Greeks in track and field techniques; and invitations went out in December 1895.

It was hardly an international event at all but rather a Greek national sports with competing guests. Two-thirds of the competitors were Greek, the Americans arrived only on the eve of the Games because no one told them that the Greek calendar adhered to the system common before everyone else changed it in the 1750's and the international muster was a mere 21 Germans, 19 Frenchmen, 14 Americans and 8 Britons decked out with a couple of Danes, Hungarians and Swiss. There were medals to be won but they were of silver-gilt because it was felt that men's lust for gold had given that particular metal a reputation too unsavoury to be associated with this semi-religious rite.

Should anyone think that narrow patriotism and anti-foreign feeling is something which has crept into the Olympics since its modern re-birth, the events at Athens should be a sad disillusionment. De Coubertin was firmly excluded from any official capacity by the Greeks who wished to run it their own way (later they fought a strong campaign against De Coubertin when he tried to insist that the Games moved around the world). The Greek Royal family, not in good odour at the time, cashed in on the Greek public interest and enthusiasm by putting in a number of semi-regal appearances to capture any publicity which was going. The Greeks got angrier and angrier as all the events they had worked and trained for were won by the Americans. The American team was split down the middle with Harvard competing against Princeton and successes for Uncle Sam taking on a very minor role. The military bearing of the Germans who stayed together, stood to attention and beat the favoured Greek gymnastics team, cast them in the role of villains of the Games and they were soundly booed at every appearance.

Victories to individuals, mostly Americans, tell of the essentially casual nature of the proceedings – James Connolly won the Triple Jump, came second in the High Jump and third in the Long Jump, and he was there although Harvard had refused him permission; the Discus was won by Robert Garrett of America and he had never handled a discus in his life before the competition started. Before leaving for Greece he had found the dimensions of a discus in a book and a Princeton friend had made one for him. Because the improvised implement was made of steel, it was far heavier than the one used in competition and he duly beat the two Greek favourites.

In the marathon, the Greeks at last got their long-awaited winner. This was Spyridon Loues, the first of three Greeks home though the third was disqualified for travelling most of the way by carriage. Loues himself was lauded by the Greek crowd, he was offered a daughter in marriage by one of the rich Greeks who had contributed towards the cost of the stadium, and awarded free drinks, shoe-shines and meals for the rest of his life – not exactly what De Coubertin had had in mind as conduct becoming to an Olympian, but concrete evidence that even in 1896 there was nothing like winning in front of a home crowd.

If Loues had fallen down en route to the stadium and an American had won that event too, the flirtation of Athens with the Olympics might have died out there and then, but because the Greeks had a hero, they were determined there would be more in the future so they did their best to take the 1900 Olympics away from Paris. De Coubertin resisted firmly though Greek persistence brought them an unofficial games in 1906 as a sop. But the Greeks were not De Coubertin's main problem – that was at home.

Back in Paris, De Coubertin's vision of a quadrennial competition for the cream of the world's youth – travelling to Athens or anywhere else to compete was by its very nature impossible for other than well-heeled aristocratic young men – was running against a quite different conception of the role of sport from the Organising Committee of the 1900 Exhibition. De Coubertin fought and pleaded for his vision, but he lost out on all counts and he was left to put the best gloss he could on all that was left of his ideals.

Instead of taking place in a convenient fortnight, the demands of the exhibition organisers, who saw it as an attendant bun-fight to the main task of attracting the world's buyers to Paris, the 'Olympic Games' became a 'Concours Internationaux Exercises Physiques et du Sport' and spread itself over the entire summer. The most unlikely events got included – fire-fighting, ballooning, pelota and angling in the Seine among them. The cruellest cut of all was that De Coubertin even failed to keep out professionals. He wrote an article in the *North American Review* in June 1900 to put the best gloss possible on the tatters left of his original conception.

> There will be target shooting, pigeon shooting, archery and shooting with the cross-bow and with firearms. For cyclists there will be a whole week of track-racing, preceded by a sensational 24 hours race. Lastly (other sections) will include motor car races, competitions of sappers and firemen, free balloon races, and trials of carrier pigeons. All this is doubtless interesting; only it is not pure sport, and for that reason I shall pass over it in this paper.

Because the German gymnasts had been so unpopular in Athens in 1896, he did his best to eliminate the idea that nation was competing against nation; and made the gymnastics open only to individual foreign gymnasts:

> ... the aim has been to avoid trouble and dispute. Gymnastic societies, to whatever country they belong, always behave in a more or less martial fashion; they march in military order, preceded by their national flag. After the troubled circumstances of late years it would be a delicate affair to unite the flags of recent opponents upon the field of contest.

However, having expressed the desirability of the competition being for man against man rather than feeding the prejudice attendant upon country versus country, he says in the very same article:

> If young men are active and in good health ... incited by the instinct of emulation, they will desire to contend, *in the name of their country,* against men of other lands.
>
> (My italics)

De Coubertin was not the clearest of thinkers, and his altruism and his French patriotism did sometimes get confused like this. He also dealt with the question of the unwelcome presence of professionals at the 1900 Olympics –

> Personally, convinced as I am that amateurism is one of the first conditions of the progress and prosperity of sport, I have never ceased to work for it ... This time, however, a

slightly different theory has prevailed . . . There will, therefore be special competitions for professionals . . . The amateurs and the professionals, without intermingling in the least, will be able to see each other at work, and comparisons advantageous to sport will be the result . . .

He makes it clear that the last sentence does not represent his own view and that he will strive to make sure that the next Games would

. . . revert to the true theory of amateurism, which declares the uselessness of the professional and desires his disappearance.

With this pious hope declared, he concluded the article by pointing to the striking way sport had spread to European nations like Germany and Sweden.

It is thus clear that sport is spreading gradually over the whole world, and taking the place of unhealthy amusements and evil pleasures in the lives of young men.

If sport was indeed having such striking moral effects, it could not be said that the Olympic Games was striking a similar blow for international harmony. The organisation at the Bois de Boulogne was chaotic, there were more competitors than spectators, races were run on turf as no cinder track was available, there were no sandpits for the jumping competitions, discus and hammer throws got caught in the trees, and the French and the Americans spent most of the time bickering. The French planned a day of athletic competition on Sunday July 15th. Many of the Americans objected on religious grounds and suggested that they were held on Saturday the 14th instead. That upset the French for whom Bastille Day was equally sacred. Late on the Saturday evening, the French decided ten finals would be held on the morrow for those whose consciences were up to it.

The Americans still won eight of the events, but college rivalries divided their team into factions for Syracuse, for Princeton and for Penn and a deal of bitterness was caused by Baxter winning the Pole Vault for Penn because other colleges' vaulters had been told not to report on the Sunday as the event would be held over. Baxter untroubled won the High Jump as well.

Ray Ewry of America won all three Standing Jump medals (High, Long and Triple), but at least one American was said to be unaware he was competing in an Olympics until he was given his medal.

De Coubertin did his best to avoid a recurrence of this general picture of chaos in 1904 and tried to get New York and Chicago in turn to play host to the Games rather than see them as another world fair side-show. He failed and at St Louis in 1904, 500 athletes turned up, nearly all Americans, with a leavening of Hungarian and German swimmers. The English universities did not know much about it, the Greeks were busy preparing for their 'unofficial' Olympics in 1906 (in reality a much more international event than the 1904 Games but one which the International Committee have never brought themselves to recognise), and the American colleges divided the spoils taking 21 of the 22 track and field medals between them. Protest and counter protest disfigured every day of competition and the marathon event produced a scandal.

At 9 miles, Fred Lorz, one of the 31 starters, got cramp, slowed down, then stopped. Some time later a car picked him up and gave him a lift back to the stadium to collect his clothes. He waved to other runners on the road as he passed them and did little to suggest that he intended the sequel. The car got cramp in turn and he jogged on alone into the stadium to be heralded the marathon champion. Foolishly he went along with the joke and took the medal (from 1900 on, gold *was* found acceptable) which got him later banned for life. Meanwhile, T. J. Hicks also of the US had kept going on the highly dangerous combination of brandy and strychnine and won the race by being the first man home without the assistance of wheels. He was too far gone to stand to take his medal.

In 1908, Italy should have been the next nation to play host to the sorry travelling circus that the first three modern Olympics had proved, but finding that they could not raise the necessary finance, they changed their mind. In their place stepped the United Kingdom who at this time were making determined efforts to woo France as a potential ally as the power of Germany continued to loom. A massive Franco-British exhibition spreading itself over 140 acres of Shepherd's Bush, a veritable 'white city' of palaces of culture and music, with cascading fountains, a giant 'flip-flap', loggia restaurants and ornamental gardens was opened by King Edward and Queen Alexandra in May. In July, the royal couple were also on hand to declare the Fourth Olympics open at the White City stadium.

The British Olympic Association had worked hard to ensure, in the limited time available for preparations once Italy withdrew, that the Games would, this time at least, run smoothly. It was a vain hope. The weather was bad, the attendance once the royal party was off the scene was poor, and ill-feeling between nation and nation and in particular between the UK and the USA was rife.

Speaking at a Dulwich College speech day in October, the ex-headmaster of Eton, Dr Warre, referred to 'the Olympic agony through which we have passed'. He went on to ask despairingly;

Do they (i.e. the Games) really bring together the nations of the world? Do they help for peace or make for trouble? The answer must be that such gatherings are pregnant with possibilities of friction . . .

The 1908 Games was not only pregnant, it was duly delivered of a bawling brood of troubles, most of them of a purely nationalistic nature. A combination of English officials with a tendency to insensitivity and arrogance, and an American team which was largely composed of athletes of Irish descent and sympathies (it is hardly necessary to add that the relations between England and Ireland were not of the sweetest at this time) was an explosive mixture.

The Games got off to a bad start when the British failed to display either the American or the Swedish flags at the stadium and ordered the Finnish team to march under the Russian flag. The Swedes protested (later they withdrew from the Games because of a wrestling decision which was not to their liking) and the Finns marched without a flag (to the great displeasure of the Russian Ambassador who was present). True to their republican traditions the Americans failed to dip their flag in salute to the Royal Box and the pattern for international disharmony was set.

One doubts that the British officials (this was the last Games at which the host nation provided all the judges) actually cheated, although the American press thought so, but their habit of using their megaphones to shout British athletes on to greater efforts did not do much for their reputation for disinterested objectivity. And that, so far as the Americans were concerned, did not survive the 400 metres. In the final, Carpenter of the US ran across the path of Halswell of GB (whether the collision was accidental or deliberate depends on whether one reads British or American accounts), and was disqualified. The race was ordered to be re-run without Carpenter but because the other American runners withdrew in protest, Halswell was left to run an Olympic final solo. Amazingly enough, he won it, but his victory put Anglo-American relations beyond patching.

Even without this accumulated ill-feeling, the marathon would have been uniquely dramatic – one of those sporting occasions rarer than is sometimes thought, of a loser's name going into history and a winner's disappearing almost into oblivion. It was the first Olympic marathon run over the now traditional distance of 26 miles 385 yards – a curious choice but one accounted for because the distance from the grounds of Windsor Castle to the White City stadium is exactly that, and that the race started at Windsor to allow the Royal children to see the 56 starters.

On the road, many runners, watched at various times by an estimated quarter of a million people, flattered only to deceive, and withdrew long before the end. News reached the stadium that at the 20 mile mark, the leader was Charles Hefferon (of South Africa but an Englishman by birth) minutes in front of the second man Dorando Pietri of Italy who in his turn was well up on a group of Americans. As often happens to a runner who has gone too fast in the middle stages, Hefferon began to go metaphorically backwards. This no one knew in the stadium, and it was a surprise when the Italian, in the last stages of collapse, was first to set foot on the track for a final lap. Dazed and stumbling he started to run around the wrong way then fell. The Americans, convinced that a 'British' runner must be second, yelled for him to be helped to his feet and pushed in the right direction while the British officials screamed at anyone who looked likely to assist the stricken Italian. At that point, news came that it was John Hayes of America who was about to come into the stadium as the second man. Both shouting parties rapidly changed their previous views. Leave him there said the Americans, pick him up said the British. The home shouts won and

Pietri was helped to his feet and half frog-marched and half-carried across the tape. The protest was inevitable and valid, Dorando had been helped, Hayes therefore was the winner. But it was Dorando who got the hero's treatment – at Queen Alexandra's request a special gold cup was made which she presented personally to him, he got a cheque, he did a guest appearance at a music hall and his effigy adorned Madam Tussaud's – in unofficial terms at least he has been the victor.

And so the Americans went home, their sportswriters to recount in detail the perfidies of treacherous Albion, and the English to reflect on the lack of gentility on the other side of the Atlantic.

Dr Warre in the speech I have already quoted gave voice to what was regrettably a common view:

> We effete Britishers, as sportsmen, mourned to see our cousins' flag disgraced before the nations of Europe, and grieved to find ourselves compelled to recognise that the Stars and Stripes was the shroud that covered International sport in a dishonoured grave.

As an epitaph to the first Games to be held in London, one must add that not only did international relations take a nose-dive, but the rigidly defined conception of the amateur was shown up for the farce it was when French cyclists were supplied with free cycles, free facilities and training expenses by British cycle firms in return for the publicity attendant upon the team using British cycles – an Edwardian overture to the troubles in ski-ing the I.O.C. would be facing in the future.

So far we have seen the early Games serving as a fruitful breeding ground for difficulties of patriotically inspired friction, of dubious amateurism, of commercial interference and of sport used for political prestige. I quote, not from a modern source but from *The Field* which greeted the plans announced for the 1908 Olympics in the following terms:

> On the whole the history of the Olympic endeavour may be taken as proof, and the new programme as tantamount to a confession, that for practical purposes amateurism is indefinable . . .

With its quasi-religious ceremonial rituals of hymns, mottos, oaths and display* all geared to enshrining amateurism and Olympian competition on a plane higher than ordinary life, the Olympics have *always* been a manifestation of hypocrisy and a vain attempt to deal with hard facts by the simple process of ignoring them. To those who would say that the Olympics are not what they were, the only truthful answer is that they never were.

And one has only to turn to the Official Report of the Olympic Games of 1912 held in Sweden to find that the besetting problem of the Games, its size, has already raised its head in common with the others.

De Coubertin had said in 1909 when the Games were awarded to Sweden that it would be a mistake to copy London which was 'too comprehensive' for

> ... The Games must be kept more purely athletic; they must be more dignified, more discreet; more in accordance with classic and artistic requirements; more intimate, and, above all, less expensive.

Fine words, but the Swedes' original plan to reduce the Games to a standard programme of athletics, wrestling, gymnastics and swimming was discounted at the I.O.C. Congress by delegates from countries who had a vested interest (*viz* a chance of medals) in the inclusion of football, shooting, yachting** etc. After two

---

*The antecedents of many of the trappings are a deal more modern than Ancient Greece and Rome. *Citius, Altius, Fortius* was borrowed by De Coubertin from the coping stone over the doorway of a French lycée run by one of his friends. The Olympic hymn was distinctly spurious. The Olympic torch and flame stem from 1936. The Olympic flag and oath were not devised until 1920 and the Olympic rings were adopted first in 1913. Also, although De Coubertin's famous dictum 'The important thing in the Olympic Games is not winning but taking part' will no doubt continue to be ascribed to him in the public mind, the real utterer was the Bishop of Pennsylvania in a 1908 sermon. If it really is more important to take part than to win, a good many millions of pounds, dollars and roubles have been wasted by the governments of the world, for if there is one driving force greater than the efforts of world powers to uphold their waning prestige with a bagful of gold medals, it must be the anxiety of emerging nations to put a gold medal seal on their recent arrival in the atlases. The important thing in the Political Games is not taking part but winning.

**The Italians were all for including ski-running as this was 'of great military importance' (!)

more attempts to keep the events and the costs down, the Swedes had to give in to a larger programme than ever. Even De Coubertin himself was no help, for after counselling intimacy he was asking the Swedes to award medals for such unlikely events as mountain ascents, game shooting and aeronautics (one would have thought he could have seen for himself firstly the impossibility of judging such events on a comparative basis, and secondly the amount of professional assistance needed from guides, gillies and mechanics, but instead the Swedes had gently to point the factors out and he in turn dropped the idea).

The other countries got their wishes generally and the poor Swedes were left with the bill. Sadly they reflected afterwards;

> The experience of the Fifth Olympiad most incontestably shows . . . there are required not only personal effort on the part of the organisers, *but also the most ample financial resources.* (My italics)

For their money, the Swedes had a satisfying Games in terms of Swedish success – before the Games took place they imported a Swedish athletics coach Erni Hjertberg who had spent forty years in the USA and English lawn tennis, rowing and swimming coaches (for whom they had advertised in English papers). They reaped the benefits for their preparations.

Any pretence that the Games were for individuals and not countries was abandoned in 'an official system of counting points'. A table awarding three points for a gold medal, two for a silver and one for a bronze was headed by the US (80 pts) but Sweden finished second (30 pts for five each of every kind of medal) marginally ahead of Finland (29 pts). Great Britain were well down the list with 15 points and that led to something of a national outcry at home when bitter post-Games inquests were held, and Britain's failures were used as proof of a national decadence and a physical deterioration of her youth. In other words, parallels were already being drawn between success as a nation and success at sport, with the inevitable corollary that national prestige depended on sportsmen. Far from there being a separation of sport and politics, the two were already bound together in the public eye all of sixty years ago. (So important was this aspect of political prestige that the Germans, who would have been hosts for the 1916 Games but for the War, had, by

1914, sent commissions to America to learn the secrets behind American successes at Stockholm, concluded that better American opportunities and facilities had much to do with it, and distributed £15,000 from the German Olympic Committee to local athletic federations to subsidise training).

Finland's Kolehmainen won the 5,000 metres in a desperately close finish with Bouin of France, breaking the world record by nearly half a minute, and went home with two other gold medals for victories in the 10,000 metres and in the 8,000 metres cross country race. In normal circumstances he would have been remembered as the Man of the Games. That honour fell to another man, like Dorando before him a loser, yet one who would be remembered long after the names of the winners of his events had been lost in obscurity. This was the American half-Indian Jim Thorpe.

Thorpe's all-round athletic ability was phenomenal. He did no training worth speaking of but he could run, throw and jump so spectacularly that in Stockholm he won the pentathlon and the decathlon as if his fellow competitors had been smitten by paralysis. Fifty years later his total of points would have still placed him first in the British decathlon rankings, which will give some indication of how far in advance of his contemporaries he was. He was presented to the Swedish King and returned to America after the Games to receive a hero's welcome and a complimentary letter from President Taft.

Thorpe was the hero of 1912, but he turned into the villain of 1913. An American newspaper printed details of his early career in sport – for $25 a week, Thorpe had played baseball for a North Carolina minor league club. The matter was taken up by the Amateur Athletic Union who wrote to the Swedish Olympic Committee in January 1913, a letter that reached its destination on February 6th. Signed jointly by the President, the Vice-President and the Secretary of the AAU, it declared that the AAU had decided that the information they had received turned Thorpe into a professional and they were resolved to return all Thorpe's prizes to the Swedish Olympic Committee. They apologised for unwittingly including a professional in their team. Of Thorpe himself, they said,

The reason why he himself did not give notice of his acts,

is explained by him on the ground of ignorance. In some justification of his position, it should be noted that Mr Thorpe is an Indian of limited experience and education in the ways of other than his own people.

The Swedish Olympic Committee took no action at all themselves other than to submit the matter to an International Olympic Committee meeting in Lausanne in May 1913. At that gathering, the forces who saw any deviation from the norm of the rich leisured amateur as something distasteful if not positively evil carried the day, Thorpe was to return his medals, and his points and records were eliminated from the record books. A more classic example of a sledgehammer used to crack a nut can hardly be imagined. Thorpe went on to become one of America's greatest ever professional football players; Bie of Norway and Wieslander of Sweden refused to take the pentathlon and decathlon medals pointing out that as far as they were concerned they had been fairly and squarely beaten in the arena and no retrospective arithmetic could change that; and posterity forgot them and instead remembered Thorpe as the greatest all round athlete of his day.

One interesting footnote to the sorry affair lingers on. Among the pentathletes and decathletes who were beaten out of sight by an illiterate Indian, was a young American athlete who specialised in the discus. He threw the discus 34.72 metres in the pentathlon only for the untrained Thorpe to hurl it 35.57 metres. The young American was Avery Brundage and in that difference of less than a metre is it not possible to see the seeds of the growth of Brundage to perhaps the most virulent hard-liner on Olympic amateurism the movement has ever known – the millionaire beaten by a man who had once taken home 25 dollars for his prowess at baseball, and unlike him could not afford to play without pay.

CHAPTER SIX

Sports for Barbarians and Philistines

One of the most striking things about historical analyses is that developments in any field of human activities seem always to have earlier foundations than are generally suspected, and that trends linger after they were thought to have become extinct. In association and rugby football, in cricket and in the Olympics, we have seen how the Edwardians were influenced by what had happened in sport before their time, and how their actions and opinions are still reflected in many of our current sporting arguments. Whatever glosses have been placed upon the Edwardian era since, unquestionably class consciousness played an enormous part in their sport. It is often said that the class system is dead. That we have come a very long way towards abolishing it since 1914 is undeniable, but rumours of its final demise have been grossly exaggerated.

It is no part of my purpose to perpetuate snobbery and class consciousness of any variety, conventional or inverted, but it would be foolish to deny that in most of our sports it is possible to see that they have taken the forms they have because of the social class of the majority of their participants. Divisions between North and South which took their most dramatic form in rugby football but which can clearly be seen in other sports, were in a hundred ways differences of class as much as of region. We have seen too, how many of the rules and laws enacted by administrations were specifically designed to keep individual sports broadly within a class, meanwhile excluding the ordinary working man.

In many cases simple economics played a large part – what Edwardian working man could have dreamed of owning golf clubs, or a squash court or a trout stream? What is extraordinary is that for most sports which have required lavish finances, a cheaper substitute has been found for the ordinary man, and for that matter for our old friend the middle class Philistine.

The propensity of the middle and working classes to mimic the upper and to follow, albeit at a distance, a pattern already set by their 'betters', is a phenomenon which would bear closer scrutiny in many other fields than sport. Nevertheless, sport being our concern here we must speak of that alone.

The rich man raced his horses, the ordinary man his whippet or his greyhound.* The rich man fished for salmon and trout, the ordinary man for perch and roach – that the ordinary man's prey is referred to as 'coarse' can hardly be accidental. The rich man raced his cars, the ordinary man his motor bike or his cycle. The rich man played Royal tennis or rackets, the Philistine came up with lawn tennis as a garden party alternative.

Lawn tennis and golf were very much Edwardian growth industries for the Edwardian middle classes took them up with a great appetite and enthusiasm. They were expensive in outlay which was welcome because it kept out the man in the street, but not so expensive as to become the preserve of the very rich.

In 1907 it was estimated that golf was providing employment for about 20,000 full time employees (stewards professionals, etc) and 80,000 part time caddies, and that in 1906 alone another 20,000 had taken up the game for the first time. It threw up its own heroes – J. H. Taylor, Harry Vardon, James Braid for example. This Edwardian 'big three'** took sixteen of the twenty-one British Opens decided between 1894 and 1914 and it was only after 1902 that they had the advantage of using the newly invented rubber-core ball. Therefore many of their scores around British courses have to be put in perspective by the knowledge that they were made without the advantage of modern club design and moreover made with the old fashioned solid gutty ball.

*Greyhound racing after a mechanical hare was first tried in England in 1876, but the first track proper was only opened at Belle Vue Manchester in 1926 after the sport had become popular and financially successful in the United States.

**Although these few could make perhaps £1,000 per annum from the game, they were also expected to fulfil all the engagements and tasks of an ordinary professional – repairing clubs, playing rounds with members, teaching etc. Small wonder, it was said, that 'their form should be subject to periods of vicissitude and distress'.

166

Tennis's major championships at Wimbledon produced their own big names although it was said in 1891 that Wimbledon would soon die as it was unable to compete with the popularity of the bicycle! Lottie Dod won her fifth women's singles in 1893. Reggie Doherty won the men's singles from 1897–1900 to be succeeded by his brother Laurie from 1902–6. Laurie Doherty also had an outstanding Davis Cup* record – from 1902 to 1906 he played seven singles matches and five doubles and won every one of them. He must have been an exceptional player, but so far as Wimbledon is concerned, winning the title was a good deal less an achievement than it was later. The reason is that the holder of the title did not have to play other than in the final itself, and could step on the court fresh to play against an opponent who had played his way through the challenge rounds. It was unfair of course, but the weight of tradition was as usual against any change. In vain did A. F. Wilding, holder of the men's title from 1910–1913 appeal to be allowed to resign his title and play through the rounds like everyone else. He was told that the ridiculous formula was 'hallowed by tradition' and that 'the championships are so successful an attraction, no alteration is thought necessary'. The holders of titles did not have to play through until 1922.

Tennis and cycling, another flourishing leisure industry, both had to face the problem of shamateurism. As more and more people took up the sport, the sales of racquets and cycles rose to meet the demand. Then as now, there was no better advertisement or endorsement for equipment than to see it used by the champions. Firms therefore found it worth their while to supply free equipment to outstanding players and cyclists and bask in the reflected glory.

Abuses in lawn tennis particularly drew much adverse comment in the press. Amateur players sometimes refused to attend a tournament unless a certain brand of ball was used, and when one firm invoiced a player for equipment supplied to him, they got the bill returned together with a letter saying that a player of his standing could hardly be expected to pay. *C. B. Fry's Magazine* carried an article on tennis in 1907 which said:

*The cup was donated by the rich father of a Harvard student Dwight Davis who played in the first match in 1900.

It is a most lamentable thing for English lawn tennis that the game should have fallen under the influence of trade interests in recent years. One has to be behind the scenes to realise the serious extent to which the suborning of persons of influence in lawn tennis has been practised.

There had been something of a scandal in 1905 at Wimbledon when the championships had been played with a non-regulation size ball. *The Field* and a New Zealand freelance journalist P. A. Vaile, both pointed out that the ambiguity of the position of Archdale Palmer who was both paid secretary of the All England Tennis Club *and* the salaried manager of Slazenger's* lawn tennis and general sports section, was not compatible with the authority's necessary reputation for independence of commercial interests. I mention this matter to show that it was not only a matter of the working man who could not afford to play unless he were paid that made the amateur an unworkable concept. Tennis was and remained for many years a sport for the middle and upper-middle classes – open public courts were just not yet available,** but pure amateurism was still an impossibility.

Tennis was a new sport and because it was largely a middle-class phenomenon it has retained a middle-class image – can there be a more typical example of English middle-class values than Wimbledon with its Centre Court crowd supporting British players first and the underdog second, and retiring to the tea-lawn for fortification at frequent intervals? This is not a criticism, merely an attempt to show that the sport has retained a particular character inevitable because of its historical background.

Where tennis was Philistine and middle-class, racing was and is inevitably Barbarian and aristocratic. It was said in 1907 that it would be difficult to imagine a more aristocratic and blue-blooded body than the Jockey Club – 'it would be easier, indeed, to upset the British Constitution than to upset the Jockey Club'. Self-elected and abrogating all authority unto itself, if the Jockey Club had not been run by aristocratic men with the independence

*This is in no way meant to reflect on Slazenger's position in sport today, merely to show that the business ethics of 1905 were not ours.
**In 1910 it was said that the very wet summer of 1909 gave an impetus to the construction of hard courts but that there were more hard courts in Hamburg alone than in the whole of England.

coming from enormous private wealth, it would never have been able to control a sport which by its very nature is wholly dependent upon the betting industry. If judges or stewards were expected to pronounce on finishes and objections in which they had a personal financial interest, the chances of getting an independent decision would be infinitesmal. Malpractices which had been common in racing in earlier centuries were stamped out, and because of the operations of the Jockey Club and the National Hunt Committee, racing was seen to be 'straight'.

Its image was enhanced further by the monarch. Edward's fortunes as a leading owner were followed eagerly by every class, as indeed the Queen's is today. Edward's first win as an owner was in 1886 with a filly called Counterpane ridden by Fred Archer, but it was his later wins that caught the public imagination. In 1896, his colt Persimmon won the Derby and the St Leger and Thais won the 1,000 Guineas and came second in the Oaks, netting him a pleasant £26,819 over the season. Persimmon also won him the Ascot Gold Cup the following season. 1898 was a relatively barren year, his much fancied two year old Diamond Jubilee showing more temper than class and taking a strong dislike to its jockey. But in 1899, as a three year old, Diamond Jubilee came good as they say. It won the 2,000 Guineas, the Derby, the St Leger and the Newmarket and Eclipse Stakes and Edward Prince of Wales finished as top owner winning nearly £30,000 with the added bonus that his Ambush II won the Grand National too. Some barren years followed but as the King of England he had the infinite pleasure of winning the Derby and the 2,000 Guineas with Minoru and was able to lead in the horse at Epsom surrounded by scenes of great enthusiasm and with shouts of 'Good Old Teddie' singing in his ears.

The popularity of racing was striking and West End theatre managements did their best to cash in on the trend by staging melodrama after melodrama with a racing background, often with a horse race on stage as part of the action. As the theatre was patronised almost exclusively by the middle classes, we can be sure that the audience was full of those anxious if only vicariously to share in the sport of Kings.

That other medium for betting, the boxing ring, did not carry the royal seal of approval. Bare-knuckle fighting, most Barbarian of spectacles, has fallen victim to Philistine Victorian respectability and was made illegal. Efforts by men like the Marquess of Queensberry to civilise the sport, and the introduction of boxing gloves, gradually brought it back to respectability. There was no official body in control of boxing until the British Boxing Board of Control was formed as late as 1929, and there was a long struggle between unscrupulous promoters who wanted no interference with their right to put hungry immigrants and the like into the ring to knock each other senseless for a pittance, and others who wanted to put the sport on a more acceptable plane. A body as undemocratic as the Jockey Club was formed in 1891 which gradually assumed control in the absence of a proper authority.

This was the National Sporting Club where the elect donned dinner jackets, lit cigars and settled down with their brandies to watch boxing contests as an after-dinner entertainment. Even the noble lineage of the Club (they used their privileged position to rule that no British championships were permitted other than on their august premises) did not preserve them from a Crown prosecution in 1901 when a boxer was killed in a fight on NSC premises. It was a test case and the last attempt by authority to make boxing illegal. Briefing Marshall Hall for their defence, the Club was found not guilty and the way was clear thereafter for the growth of the sport.

In imitation of the National Sporting Club, less exalted premises, from Wonderland and the Blackfriars Ring down to the humble East End swimming baths, staged their own promotions and half a dozen professional bills a week was common. From the start of modern boxing, there were no British boxers who could match the heavyweights of America – and it would take a careful examination of national diets to find the reasons – but the halls and the booths threw up many a brilliant individual at the lighter weights. Jim Driscoll, Joe Bowker, Jimmy Wilde, Ted Kid Lewis and Freddie Welsh and many others grew in so fertile a soil. And in 1909, Lord Lonsdale did his bit for humanity in boxing by introducing the famous Lonsdale Belt for competitors at fixed weights from Heavy to Fly (eight stone and under).

One would love to examine other sports in detail too for each in its way contributes something unique to the progress of what we call sport. Some, like aviation, yachting, ski-ing and motor racing were prohibitively expensive for anyone other than the affluent few. Others, like hockey and rowing chose deliberately to remain exclusive lest they had a growth comparable to soccer and rugby and had to face the difficulties posed by the entry of the man who could not always afford to play. The Amateur Rowing Association ruled quite firmly that no man could be an amateur if he was a 'manual or menial worker' in any trade at all! On this ground, which does have a sort of nightmare logic about it, the American Olympic sculler J. B. Kelly was rejected from Henley although he had won the 1920 Olympic title, on the grounds that he had been a bricklayer. (Kelly had the last laugh however for if his humble trade was not aristocratic enough for the Henley Committee, it was certainly acceptable in rather higher Royal circles when his daughter Grace became the Princess Grace of Monaco on her marriage to Prince Rainier.) In equestrianism too something of the same order prevailed, for it was not until after the Second World War that any military rider other than a full officer was recognised as an amateur. Time and again one comes back to this thorny subject in sport after sport. Not, however, that it was a British problem alone.

Life magazine in 1907 was making it clear that college sport in the United States was facing its own difficulties:

So long as college games were of restricted interest, and brought in no revenue, and were almost altogether played by lads who, 'gentleman' like, did not have to support themselves, and had leisure to play, this question of amateur standing made no particular trouble. But with the increasing publicity and importance of the games, their awful progress in revenue-earning capacity, the momentous growth in their tax upon the time and energies of the players, and the aggravated solicitude about winning, has come this searching for husky, hard-working youths to play in them, and this feeling on the part of some of the youths thus employed that the labourer, whose efforts contribute to the acquisition of big sums of gate money, is worthy of his hire. And so the commercial standard, which governs the great world of business and most of the practical concerns of life, keeps elbowing its way into college sports, and trying to drive the 'gentleman's' standard out.

171

I quote the paragraph at length because it encapsulates the dilemma that all sport has had to face – that once it became of more than passing interest to player or spectator, it became a sphere of human activity subject to all the economic and social forces to be found elsewhere. The greater its following, the greater its importance. The greater its importance, the greater its attraction for those who would use it either for commercial gain or personal aggrandisement. Also, the greater its importance, the greater its attraction for use in political propaganda.

In Edwardian times, all these developments can be seen firmly underway. With the exception of drugs which had not yet been invented and therefore could not be used in sport,* there seems no modern sports problem which does not have an Edwardian predecessor. Foul play, defensive tactics, crowd misbehaviour, reactionary administrations, law changes to attract crowds, narrow patriotism, exploitation of players, press sensationalism, too much stress on winning, snobbery, commercial interference, bribery, fixed results for betting interests, ghosted books and articles, inadequate and dangerous facilities, may all sound very modern but the Edwardians knew all about them too.

The inescapable conclusion is that sport is not and never has been 'special'. It can lay no claims to being conducted on a higher plane than the rest of existence, but like the rest of life has its good and its bad alike, and we do sport a disservice to pretend otherwise. At a personal level of one man against another, chivalry and unselfishness do have a way of breaking through. In the Olympics chapter, I showed how much friction had been caused by international sport. To redress the balance, it would be possible to show hundreds of instances in Olympic competition where sport has brought men of different creeds, races or ideologies together and cemented long lasting individual friendships. Similarly there is always something heart-warming in the personal relationships between say, David Watkins and Colin Meads, or Bobby Moore and Pélé. At this individual level, international or social relationships have never presented any problem – it is when individual identities are submerged in class, club, region or country ones that frictions start, but it is pre-

---

*On the other hand how can one describe Hicks' Olympic marathon win on brandy and strychnine, or drinking champagne at half time in a Cup Final, other than as uses of artificial stimulants?

172

cisely those group identities which give spice to most of sport's major competitions.

It will be remembered that the popular newspapers and modern sport grew up together in Edwardian times feeding off each other and gaining mutual benefit in their phenomenal growths. The popular press has always been a target, often rightly, for its habit of dwelling on the sensational and for appealing broadly to the baser instincts of man. Certainly, sport is sometimes damaged by press sensationalism. If a hundred thousand people attend a football match and one hooligan amongst them attacks a referee, anyone who saw the headlines next day could be forgiven for thinking that football was going to the dogs and conveniently forgetting that 99,999 people had spent a harmless afternoon out. To place another matter in perspective, one has to remember too that the heralding of some non-event in boxing as the potential Fight of the Century can sometimes be put down to the fact that the billing is very much to the benefit of the journalist himself, who will be persuading his editor that he must fly the necessary thousands of miles to cover the event with all expenses paid.

To these common criticisms there is of course an effective and powerful answer. It is that sensational copy sells newspapers. Proprietors, editors, journalists etc are not in the business to educate the population at large, they are supplying a service for which there is a demonstrable demand. More people wish to read about a footballer's drinking habits than wish to read a technical analysis of his team's patterns of play. More people wish to read Desmond Hackett's xenophobic despatches of football as international warfare, than Brian Glanville's attempts to lift eyes beyond the horizon of the bob bank.

I said at the beginning of the book that history could perhaps help us to see the nature of some of the modern problems of sport, but I also said that history did not necessarily present us with the answers. What however I hope has emerged from this book is that fundamentally sport, because it is not something special, is subject to all the pressures of the society in which it takes place. Modern sport is what it is, for good and for ill, because it is what we have made it. We get the sport and the sporting press we deserve. It is our creation and if we wish to change it, ultimately we can do so.

If a football team wins its matches by crippling its opponents it is able to do so only as long as people are prepared to pay out good money to see them do it. If a newspaper devotes two-thirds of its report of a football match to a round by round description of blows exchanged between a centre half and a centre forward, it will only do so as long as people show by buying the paper that that is what they wish to read.

The governing bodies of our major sports have for too long treated the general public as people whose presence is at best tolerated. Compared with the legendary difficulties of selling refrigerators to Eskimos, what better assignment could any salesman be given than to be asked to sell sport to the British? In the coming years every sport will be facing severe competition from all the multitude of channels opening up for a man's time and money as leisure and affluence continue to increase. Instead of resting content with what was once a monopoly position of a supply of cheap entertainment, and happy to put up with even bad publicity if it brought the crowds in, administrations are going to find in the future that they will have to work hard even to stay in the same place.

In America, football, basketball and baseball have come to terms with the necessity of selling sport to the public. When a man pays his money, he is treated well, kept fully informed of what is happening during play and generally treated like a human being whose presence is welcome and who it is hoped will be along at the next home game. One has only to think of the parallel experience at the average football match or athletics meeting in this country to get the point.

Together with this drive to sell British sport to the British, there would be an opportunity for the administrations to promote what they considered to be the best aspects of their sport. If they could grasp that anything they can do to create an informed and knowledgeable public is in their interests, and that the more discriminating the public the better it is for the sport, then they would be on the way to making some progress.

The Edwardians left us many a problem, as we have seen in our examination of various sports, but they had one thing which perhaps we have since lacked. This is a sense that sport above all else was something to be enjoyed. Mixed up with the snobbish attitude that a man who played for money was some sort of inferior being, there was also the healthier opinion that the rewards which could be won from sport were not worth the price that had to be paid if that price was devoting one's life solely to sport. There is a contemporary danger that success in sport at the highest level will be wholly restricted to those who close their eyes to all that life has to offer outside the field of play. Certainly a spectator who has paid his money at the gate is entitled to see players striving to the utmost to win a game – to do otherwise is an insult to the crowd and the opponents alike. On the other hand, we have to make a conscious effort to retain a sense of perspective. For a British team to lose an international match does not mean that the country's youth has fallen into physical and moral decline any more than a win means that Pax Britannica still holds sway over half the territories of the world.

We saw how the Edwardian public school obsession with sport produced a whole class of men trying so desperately to become 'manly' that they remained boys all their lives. It would be tragic if we fell into a similar trap and by placing too much store on sporting success lapsed into a perpetual immaturity. It is up to us as a nation to decide at what point the price becomes too high. Edgar Joubert, the French sportswriter who I have quoted elsewhere, once said this – 'the over-rating of sport stems from an inferiority complex'. It seems all too often that British sportsmen are expected to prove the superiority of all things British by their actions off the field of play. We have to come to the realisation that a victory on the field is just that. The winning of the Jules Rimet trophy in perpetuity or trunkfuls of gold medals at every Olympics, are not going to restore the days when Britain ruled half the world and it is both idle, spurious and dangerous to pretend it does.

Much of the elevation of Edwardian times to a lost golden age is misplaced because the nostalgia conceals the very real turbulence beneath the surface. By 1910–12, a kind of desperate rigidity to change had set in because change threatened stability of morals, religion and the Empire. Conflicts between old orders and the new broke out in many different fields – the Liberals and the House of Lords, struggles to reform the army and the navy, unions and employers, Irish home rule and Ulster, the fight for women's suffrage to name only the major ones. The outbreak of the First World War did not bring an end to the gracious

Edwardian age, the seeds of self-destruction were already present and if it had not been for the outbreak of the War, there would in all probability have been a social explosion instead.

Sport can only be a small part of society, and as such it is governed by prevailing social morals and ideologies. One would suggest that Britain as a country has yet to find a realistic world role compatible with her relative weakness in natural resources, and lingering Edwardian-like reluctance to recognise unwelcome facts has meant that so necessary a process has been for too long delayed. Britain was first in the field in industrialisation but her superiority was temporary and has long since vanished. Britain was first in the field in most major sports too, but that superiority was also temporary.

Unfortunately, because sport has had so overwhelming an attraction to the population at large, and because we continue to produce men of talent, it has been possible to deceive ourselves with the comforting notion that whatever the failings of British industry, at least we can still put the foreigners in their place on the field of play. And, as a result, sportsmen, including rugby players and athletes who remain strictly part-timers, when they don a British vest are expected to absolve all the deficiencies of a nation. If they prove mortal and fail, they are then handed the hair shirts we were not prepared to wear ourselves, and castigated for not training or trying hard enough. Sporting crowds can be kind, but just like their Edwardian counterparts they can be cruel too. In simple justice, the least we can do is to finally abolish the outmoded concept of the amateur in all sports and see to it that our sportsmen at least get the rate for the job we seem to be asking them to do.

The lot of the Edwardian professional sportsman was not generally a happy one, but before we close this survey we must have a brief look at another large group of second-class citizens – women. The position of women in Edwardian sport, to be fully documented, would make this book half as long again, but we cannot complete a picture of Edwardian sport without some awareness of their disabilities.

As women were gradually freed from the tyranny of the Victorian drawing-room, they looked more and more to the outdoors and indulged in archery, cycling, skating and golf though the formality of their dress precluded much in the way of strenuous competition. There were no women's events included in the Olympics until 1928 but there were ladies' events in tennis from 1884 on, in skating from 1906 on, in hockey from 1902 on and in badminton from 1900 on. By 1905 many sporting magazines were carrying features like 'The Sportswoman' or 'The Outdoor Girl'. It became fashionable among society ladies to claim some sporting accomplishment or other – Ellaline Terris was known to be a shot and a motorist, Zena and Phyllis Dare played golf, Ethel Irving went fishing as indeed did Princess Alexandra, but the glamour of the names should not conceal the very real prejudice that existed against women at the time. For such illustrious women, indulgence in sport could be seen as a kind of charming foible, but it would be a disaster if the ordinary wife and mother were to mimic them.

Two of the major sports magazines of the time show conclusively what form male reactions to this new breed of sporting women took. *Badminton Magazine* had this to say in 1900:

(For women) ... beauty of face and form is one of the chief essentials, but unlimited indulgence in violent outdoor sports, cricket, bicycling, beagling, otter-hunting, paper-chasing, and – most odious of all games for a woman – hockey, cannot but have an unwomanly effect on a young girl's mind, no less than her appearance ... Let young girls ride, skate, dance and play lawn tennis and other games in moderation, but let them leave field sports and rough outdoor pastimes to those for whom they are naturally intended – men.

Equally chauvinistic if more complacent was *Baily's Magazine* five years later:

Truly the emancipation of women is to those who reflect on the days that are past a revalation. They have their own London clubs, bridge clubs, their hockey, tennis, golf, croquet clubs – yes, and even their rowing clubs ... Surely our ladies are inclined to indulge their individual fancies to extremes! (But fortunately) ... there are still among us ... a good sprinkling of true women, who have not bowed the knee to these mannish ways and nobly set the fashion of ladylike behaviour in sport.

The trouble, as one of the very best of historians* of the era has put it so beautifully, was that

> Just as discussions on racial integration tend to be reduced in opening arguments to the question of one's daughter marrying a negro, so discussions of women's rights over the Edwardian years tended to dissolve into emotional questions of sexual purity and motherhood.

It was in precisely these emotional terms that the two most flagrant discriminations against women – the divorce laws and the lack of a vote – were discussed. Those two issues lie outside the world of sport. However, because sport was such an outpost of male chauvinism and something of a masculine symbol, when the women's suffrage movement had failed with every democratic attempt to get its voice heard, it was sport which had to bear the brunt of the suffragettes' turn to militancy and violence. Throughout 1913, bowling greens, golf clubs, cricket grounds and football grounds had their turf torn up and damaged and their buildings burnt down, all over the country. And it was at a sports event that the movement found a spectacular martyr.

On the 4th of June 1913, the Derby field swept around Tattenham Corner with the King's horse Amner in the lead. As it did so, a member of the Women's Social and Political Union, a Miss Emily Davison, ducked under the rails and threw herself under the horse's hoofs for horse, woman and jockey to finish on the turf in a writhing heap. Symbolically, in the stand the Queen afterwards inquired after Miss Davison's health, the King after the horse and jockey (they escaped injury). Miss Davison died from her injuries and the women's movement had its martyr.

The incident, and Miss Davison's funeral procession, which was followed to St George's Bloomsbury by 6,000 women, got maximum coverage in the newspapers of the day which in a way brings us full circle. Miss Davison's use of a sporting event to bring publicity to an unpopular cause was surely the Edwardian predecessor of the tragic events at Munich in 1972 with which this book began. And so long as sport continues to attract a major share of our attention, who can know what the future has in store?

*Samuel Hynes in *The Edwardian Turn of Mind*.

Index

Index